I0762580

40 DAYS TO MOVE PAST LONELINESS
AND FIND YOUR COMMUNITY

The Friendship Devotional

Bailey T. Hurley

Contents

Tending 53

Pruning 93

Blooming 135

Closing Thoughts 176

Before You Begin

Hi, friend!

My name is Bailey, and I'm so glad you picked up this book. You may be thinking, *Glad? That's not how I feel about needing a book on how to be a friend.* Believe me, I get it. I understand it's difficult at any stage of life to feel as if you have reached a limit on how you can grow as a friend.

Friendship can be like an untended garden, with a mess of tangled weeds and exposed roots creating obstacles on the path to the areas that are blooming. In an effort to rival the perfect gardens everyone else seems to have, you might be tempted to haphazardly scatter seeds of friendship all over the place in the hopes that *something* will sprout. The problem is that not all soils are created equally, and some won't be equipped to enable a relationship to fully thrive. So how should we approach our friendships? Well, as a type-A, have-a-plan kind of girl, I have some ideas, and I'm inviting you into my process of navigating the complexities of adult friendship and sowing the seeds of God's Word into our interactions to cultivate a lifetime of care for our friends.

Before we go any further, though, I want to say that you are not the first person who has ever wondered, *What am I doing with my friendships?* You are also not the first to wish for deeper or more friendships. Nor are you the first to feel alone or left out. Many of us might say we left behind the need to be popular in middle school, but I think most of us still want to be someone's favorite friend. Friendship is a universal need, but it is also a universal struggle. We know friendship is integral for a healthy life, but figuring out how to excel in it or even do it right can feel like another goal that hasn't quite made it to reality. Social media adds another layer of frustration, since it allows us to see the picture-perfect relationships other people have without any of the problems. All these internal insecurities and external pressures can create a seemingly impossible standard in regard to contentment and the way we thrive in our friendships.

As someone who has built my ministry around cultivating and nurturing friendships (and who has walked in these trenches myself), I understand the struggle all too well. I'll never forget the time I spoke at a small church in Longmont, Colorado, and received this question from a woman during the Q and A: *I want all this friendship stuff you are talking about, but how do I know how to make the first step, especially when I'm navigating multiple friendships in different stages?*

Maybe you've wondered the same thing or something similar. Or maybe you're just desperate for any type of friendship at all, and picking up this devotional was a last resort. Regardless of how you're coming to this book, let me squeeze your hand and reassure you that no one has discovered the secret to doing friendship perfectly. But let me also tell you that cultivating solid and intentional friendships is a skill that can be practiced and honed. Over the next forty days, we'll explore several practical ways to do just that.

How to Use This Devotional

As the woman in Longmont realized, no two friendships are the same, and we may have as many as a dozen friendships at one time that are all in different stages. You might have a new acquaintance you're hoping to grow closer to, a casual friend at work you would like to invite into your social circle outside work, and a high school friend you love but who lives far away. Just as each of these relationships is unique, the needs and values in each one are also unique.

Think of it like this: In a garden, some plants are more mature than others. Some need pruning to bring them back to life. Bulbs need to be planted. Seeds won't even show signs of green for months to come.

In a similar way, we may have mature friendships that are healthy and steadily growing, friendships that require cutting back or pruning, and friendships that will take special care and months of attention and work in the hope that they will sprout. In a single morning, we might find ourselves experiencing the joy of a quality conversation with one friend while also questioning another friend's lack of response to a text message. We might desire greater depth in one friendship and more boundaries in another. Thankfully, God meets us in the complexity and variety of our friendships. He knows we are not two-dimensional characters who can find a simple solution to *every* friend hiccup at the end of each day. Instead, He gives us His Word, encouragement, grace, and very specific wisdom to guide us as we do the meaningful—and sometimes lonely—ministry of friendship.

Using the garden metaphor, this devotional is split into four sections that reflect different stages of a plant's growth. Each section has devotions, reflection questions, and unique prayers.

- The **Planting** section provides inspiration for the heavy-lifting season of making new friends. These devotions will spur you on through the weariness, frustrations, or doubts you might experience at the beginning of new friendships.
- The **Tending** section offers encouragement and practical advice for moving new friendships into greater depths and turning them into lasting relationships.

- The **Pruning** section offers advice for the difficult moments of insecurity, conflict, or disappointment. Some friendships might even need to end, and when that happens, we need God's truth to cover the hurt and sense of loss we might feel. If you find yourself encountering a hard season in your friendships, this section will help you prune and maybe remove any wilted relationships that are hindering growth or wellness.
- The **Blooming** section, meant for friendship celebrations, allows you to pause and recognize the friendship "gifts" God has given you. The prayers and prompts in this section will guide your heart toward a season of gratitude and contentedness for the friends already in your life.

Depending on where you are in your friendships, you might want to skip around the devotional and zero in on the sections that offer the best advice for what you need right now. Or you can read through the devotional from beginning to end. Along the way, you will find practical **"friendspiration" tips** and **friend date ideas** to help you foster deeper connections. Implement these as you go or flip to the ones that sound particularly curated for your friend group. Overall, I hope that the devotions and the fun extras spark personal growth and meaningful moments with current and future gal pals!

Blessing

Whether you're a recent graduate hoping to form the types of friendships you had in college, a newly remote employee wondering how you're supposed to meet people while working from home, or a single mom juggling work and daycare while longing to have an adult conversation for once, your friendship challenges will be unique to you, and my prayer is that this devotional leads to growth not only in your varied seasons of friendship but also in your relationship with the Lord, your first and truest Friend.

I NO LONGER CALL YOU SERVANTS, because a servant does not know his master's business. Instead, I have called you friends, for everything that I learned from my Father I have made known to you. You did not choose me, but I chose you and appointed you so that you might go and bear fruit—fruit that will last—and so that whatever you ask in my name the Father will give you. This is my command: Love each other.

—JOHN 15:15-17

Planting

Remember this: Whoever sows
sparingly will also reap sparingly,
and whoever sows generously will
also reap generously.

—2 CORINTHIANS 9:6

Sow your seed in the morning,
and at evening let your hands not be idle,
for you do not know which will succeed,
whether this or that,
or whether both will do equally well.

—ECCLESIASTES 11:6

Starting from Scratch

Therefore welcome one another as Christ has welcomed you, for the glory of God.
—ROMANS 15:7, ESV

No matter what age or stage of life you're in, there will come a time when you look around and realize you're surrounded by a wave of new faces rather than the comfortable familiar ones you've known. For me, the shift seemed to happen overnight. After seven years of building solid relationships in Denver, I woke up one morning to text a friend for a girls' night only to remember that my closest girlfriends had all moved away. Within the span of a year, the entire community I had spent years investing in had turned over, and I had no one to reach out to.

Movement and change are givens when it comes to life in general and friendships in particular. Just when you think you've settled into a group of friends, someone gets a new job, has a baby, or decides to relocate across the country. These and other changes might then compel you to make new friends in new circles.

In the weeks after I realized we needed to start over in our friendships, my husband (Tim) and I were forced to reflect on the ones we still had—and to reassess how we approached friendships in general. Maybe we needed a new perspective—a fresh understanding beyond the "one and done" friend date idea. Instead of trying to gather a few select people and control every possible angle to maintain those friendships forever, how could we have an open-handed posture toward anyone God might place in our lives in any given season? How could we always remain on the lookout for new friends . . . no matter how "settled" we felt with the ones we already had?

One secret to making new friends is to form a habit of welcoming new people into your circle. Be a lifelong friendship-maker. Those who keep their circle open will be the least likely to feel the effects of friendship transitions. If we are malleable to the change, we won't fall apart when friends leave and new ones require more attention. That's how Tim and I carried ourselves out of our friendship rut. We started investing in some of our acquaintances, rekindled friendships we hadn't previously made time for, and started inviting new people to connect. We didn't want our discouragement to keep us from exploring new friendships.

Starting over is hard and opening yourself up to new people is a risk, but by keeping our hands open, we remain ever ready for new "friendship gifts" God may place in front of us. When we remember how we have been welcomed by God first, we can be a welcoming presence to others. We can take His example of a generous welcome and use it to find space in our own hearts for new friends and communities.

So if you think your friendship garden is full, consider where you might make space for new seeds that may fall along your path.

Reflect

Who in your life could you see yourself extending an invitation to or wanting to know better?

Prayer

Lord, I am nervous to make new friends, because I am afraid of the risk and time it takes to open myself up to new people. I'm also still wrestling with disappointment, because I miss my old friends. Give me patience in waiting for acquaintances to turn into friendships. Thank You, Lord, for extending a welcome to me. Please strengthen and embolden me and fill me with Your joy so that I can pour into this process of making new friends. Amen.

Friendspiration

MAKING NEW FRIENDS

Here are two things to remember when making new friends:

Be specific and politely forward with your requests:

"Can I sit with you?"

"Could I get your number to connect later?"

"Would you want to go to this gym class with me?"

Follow through with your plans.

WHEN YOU'RE AFRAID *to Make the First Hello*

I will be their God,
and they will be my people.
—JEREMIAH 31:33

Social anxiety can take on many forms. Since I enjoy lots of friend time, people are often surprised to hear that I can become paralyzed in a big group of people I don't know very well—or even in a big group of people I *do* know well. Making small talk or inserting myself into an already established circle of friends can be intimidating. Perhaps you relate.

Whether approaching a new social situation or an environment where you've been numerous times, you might feel insecure about going up to people and saying hello. After all, what if you try to strike up a conversation and they ignore you? What if you say something wrong or embarrassing? What if they start discussing something you know nothing about? Believe me, I've lived those types of experiences a time or two. Being in those situations certainly doesn't do any favors for building social confidence.

Awkwardness aside, one thing I *have* learned about initiating friendship over the years is that putting myself out there always results in some kind of return. Even when the "hello" is met with rejection, it helps me see that maybe that friend group wasn't the right fit for me. But most of the time, when I gather the courage to make words come out of my mouth, I'm met with smiles, because people appreciate being seen. That initial interaction can be as simple as being the first to give a compliment or asking someone to join your book club. It might not amount to any life-changing conversations or new best friends, but at least you and the other person will receive the warm, fuzzy feeling of connection.

Don't get me wrong: Being the initiator can be intimidating, but we can muster the courage to pay that hello forward when we remember how God called us by name and invited us to be His people. Because I am seen and accepted by God, I can worry less about my fears of rejection and focus on how I can help the other person feel just as seen as I feel by God. And while some of these initiated conversations may lead to only a momentary meeting of two women sharing a brief glimpse of God's care, others might result in solid friendships!

We all want to be invited into connection. When I attend events where I don't know many people, what I really want is for someone to come over and strike up a friendly conversation with me to ease my social discomfort of being alone. But what I do instead is put on a brave face (aka look approachable and confident and act like I belong), create some good conversation starters, and ask new friends to accompany me to the snacks (because who doesn't love snacks?). So when you feel your anxieties begin to grow, remember how it feels when someone makes an effort to greet you. One small moment of bravery could be the catalyst for a deep and lasting relationship.

Reflect

How might God be drawing you out of your social anxiety and asking you to make the first step of faith by initiating conversation with someone new?

Prayer

Lord, I freeze up when I see an opportunity to introduce myself, because I am so afraid of small talk or the conversation drying up after the initial hello. I am fearful of rejection. Help me to trust that my efforts will grow into the fruit of real connection. Amen.

Friendspiration

CONVERSATION STARTERS THAT WORK

When introducing myself to new people for the first time, here are a few conversation starters I keep in my back pocket:

Anything related to a self-care routine

If it's early in the morning: What sort of tricks do you have to help yourself wake up and start the day?

If it's evening: I just started a new nighttime rhythm, but I'm not sure I love it. What do you do at night to get ready for bed?

Anything related to the town or city

If someone is new to your town: What has surprised you about living here? What do you miss about where you used to live? What are some cultural differences you've noticed? How is community prioritized differently here than where you're from?

If someone has lived in the current city a long time: What is your favorite part about living here? What hidden gems would you recommend? What is one thing you wish you could change about this city? What would you tell someone who's just moved here?

Anything related to the context of your meeting

What inspired you to come to this gathering tonight? You've been a part of this organization for a long time—how has it been meaningful to you and your family? What is the main reason you joined this group?

First Impressions

Be kind and compassionate to one another.

—EPHESIANS 4:32

In grade school, we learn never to judge a book by its cover because the story inside might be more than what the cover suggests. In the same way, we shouldn't judge others by first impressions. Few people have the confidence to be fully themselves during early encounters, and if we write someone off from a single experience alone, we might miss the opportunity to invite an incredibly unique person into our lives.

As someone who is shy around new groups of people, I am especially grateful for those who offer me the gift of a second or even third impression. Since I can take a while to warm up in unfamiliar environments, people who don't know me might view my initial quiet as unfriendliness or even coldness. In truth, I have a very bubbly spirit and would hate for others to judge me based on one interaction.

For some, being open and relatable is easy. For others, feeling safe enough to share our real life with a new person takes longer. We all have varying levels of comfort when entering friendships, and each of us has a different definition of what it means to truly connect with another person in a genuine way. For one person, a head nod from across the room might be equivalent to someone

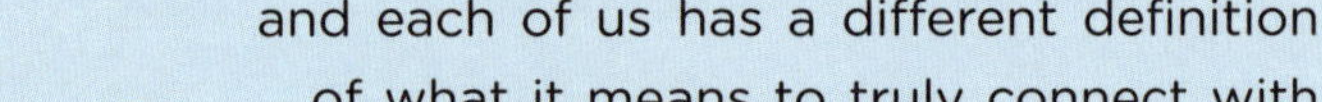

else's big hug and friendly greeting. But when we assign our own definitions of friendliness to other people or misinterpret a person's level of engagement, we might be tempted to prejudge them or write them off as unfriendly or withdrawn.

To avoid misjudging new acquaintances in this way, we can approach first-time (or even second-time) interactions with grace and openness. Stepping fully into another person's story requires patience, understanding, and time, but the extra effort is worth it if the result is unearthing a hidden gem of a friend.

When meeting new people, give them a few chances to surprise you before you decide the friendship isn't a good fit. Even if you're a stickler for punctuality and a new friend arrives late, reach for grace before judgment and consider how arriving on time may have been out of that person's control. Or if someone says something you disagree with, reach for curiosity instead of anger and search for ways to understand how that person's worldview may differ from yours. Or if the new girl is really quiet the first time you meet her, remember that she might still need and want a friend to ask the right questions and discover the well of wisdom within her. In all things, strive to give others the gift of another impression. After all, wouldn't you want the same?

Reflect

When has a first impression of someone else led you to prejudge them? Or when have you felt judged based on a first encounter? To whom might you offer the chance for a second impression?

Prayer

Lord, as I meet new people, help me to keep an open mind toward those who may not initially be easy to connect to. Give me a compassionate heart for a new friend who might need a second chance. Since there's always more to a person than what's on the surface, Lord, give me wisdom to discern good friendships when I come across them. Amen.

DRIVE-THRU

MATERIALS: a car and a good playlist

PREP TIME: 5 minutes

DATE TIME: 30–60 minutes

FRIENDS NEEDED: 1

It might not be a big, color-coordinated, Instagrammable event, but taking a scenic drive with a good playlist and slushie beverage can be the perfect setting for chatting about all the important and unimportant things of life. Some of my most memorable friend dates have been driving with the windows down, on our way to grab slushies. Whether I was twelve years old in the back seat of my mentor's car chatting with her and my best friend about faith and boys, or thirty-two years old with my own kids in the back seat as I listen to a friend share about mortgages or aging parents, deep-talk drives have become one of my favorite ways to connect with close friends.

The drive-thru date is spontaneous and special. You never know—toasting with Styrofoam slushie cups to hard days or little wins might change your entire day. So be on the lookout for that extra hour in your day, or call a friend while you drive by her house and ask, "Hey, want to go get a slushie with me right now or in thirty minutes?" Once your plans are secured, pick up your friend and ask her what her favorite songs are to sing out loud. Blast them on the radio and then grab a drive-thru treat to serve as the side for any deep (or not so deep) conversations that might spring up. The friendship endorphins that arise from this type of spontaneous hangout are definitely better than any doom-scrolling or show-bingeing you might do otherwise.

Refueling Your Friend Tank

Rising very early in the morning, while it was still dark, [Jesus] departed and went out to a desolate place, and there he prayed.

—MARK 1:35, ESV

In a typical week, we have about thirty people come over for meals, playdates, and small group. We genuinely love having people in our home and making it seem warm and inviting despite the five messy people who live in it (not to mention the cat who likes to tear through all the toilet paper in the house).

But we have our limits.

I usually am tipped off to that limit whenever I feel a disconnect from the rest of my family. Or when I experience the stress and weight of making a meal for someone when I barely have time to shop for groceries for myself. Or when I start answering my husband's questions with one-word responses (he tells me I have a "voice" I use when I'm tapped out). When these flags of overcommitment start waving in my periphery, I know I need a break. They serve as signals reminding me of the importance and value of keeping one day sacred for resting with God and my inner circle. Without our weekly Sabbath, or day of rest, we would soon be unable to function—much less host others in our space.

Sabbath should, among other things, act as our guardrail against overextending ourselves. This gift of rest allows us to set aside time when we aren't packing our schedules with events, picking up after kiddos, or washing an endless pile of dishes. It's about refueling our spirits through intentional rest and worship. Sabbath can also ground us to *why* we practice hospitable friendship in the first place. After all, spending time with God is the foundation for doing the ministry work of making and maintaining friends.

Even Jesus—the all-powerful Son of God—understood the human reality of having limits. Though His ministry revolved around healing, helping, and loving people, He also carved out space to be with His Father. Spending focused time with God allowed Him to do all the things God had planned for Him to do. He knew the value of being filled up before He could pour out.

Even more so for us, building new friendships requires a lot of output and time. You may send texts with offers to hang out, only to strike out with everyone's varied schedules. You may host people for a meal but never receive an invitation in return. You may connect well with someone who says they want to know you better but who never follows up. Having the endurance to keep going after setbacks can feel impossible when you depend on your own strength, which is why taking Sabbath rest and drawing strength from God is so important. Only God can equip you with every good thing to do His will (Hebrews 13:21), including being a friend.

So before you pour yourself out to serve or love others in your community, consider your own spiritual, emotional, physical, and mental health. Notice where you are feeling burned out, cynical, or bitter, and consider how you might be bringing this into your friendships. Pay attention if you reach a point when friend time feels less like a joy and more like an obligation. You might need to take a step back before you can be fully present to those around you. And that's okay!

Thankfully, when you live from a place of fullness and completeness in God, you're able to draw from a deeper well of love for others, no matter what obstacles you encounter. Disappointments and setbacks will happen, but by rooting your strength in the Lord, you will be able to maintain the capacity needed to keep reaching out. Remember, keeping your "yes" to God equips you to give an overall "yes" in your friendships.

Friendspiration

TIME WITH GOD

Shifting our priorities is easier said than done. One way you can ensure time with God is by creating an appointment on your calendar for Him, just like you would for a friend. I schedule these times with God three days in a row either by waking up earlier or swapping it with something else I already have on my calendar like going to the gym or watching a weekly reality show. I can always come back to those things later, and I would rather prioritize spending time with God so I can grow closer to Him and become a better friend to others.

Reflect

What keeps you from taking time to be alone with God, and what small step can you take today to add a Sabbath practice to your weekly routine?

Prayer

Lord, I confess I often choose distractions over spending quality time with You. But I know I cannot give to my friends what I don't have to give. Please help me redirect my focus toward You. Let me be filled by Your love and acceptance. And may Your love compel me to be a friend who loves and accepts others. Amen.

Finding Good Friends

The fruit of the Spirit is love, joy, peace, patience, kindness, goodness, faithfulness, gentleness, self-control.

—GALATIANS 5:22–23, ESV

Do you ever get overwhelmed at the process of constantly starting at the beginning of new friendships? Do you ever throw yourself all in on meeting new people only to find out soon after that the friendships aren't quite worth it—either because the people you're engaging with aren't as invested as you are or because you don't feel comfortable going deeper with them?

I remember meeting so many new people my first month of college. As fun as it was, I also became overwhelmed by the volume of new acquaintances, and I struggled to identify which relationships to devote my time to. As a result, I spent a lot of months bouncing from friend group to friend group trying to find my place and never really planting any seeds for friendships beyond study buddies.

Post-college life can prove to be even more difficult in regard to identifying good and solid friends to invest in. How do we discern who we make time for and how much to open up? How do we know we are saying "yes" to the right invitations? How do we know if a friendship is going to go a long way or if this specific person will be a good fit for our certain brand of quirkiness?

If you're not careful, this season of making new friends can come with its own kind of fatigue. Your response to the fatigue shouldn't be giving up on making new connections but simply taking a step back and asking yourself the important questions: *What qualities have I enjoyed in my past friendships? What qualities am I looking for in friends today? And how am I able to show up as a friend to others in this season?*

One way to practice wisdom when meeting new people is to know and identify ahead of time your definition for what makes a good friend. Creating a new definition for friendship can ease some of the hurt we feel due to any past failed friendships or the struggle we might experience in having the desire to try again.

As a follower of Jesus, you will likely want your friendships to embody certain qualities: love, joy, peace, patience, kindness, goodness, gentleness, faithfulness, and self-control, for example. Obviously, none of us can ever hope to be perfect in all these areas, but knowing which qualities are especially important can serve you well in knowing which friendships to pursue. Of course, you can also look out for fun similarities or shared interests such as which shows you both watch, what activities you enjoy, or what things you're both passionate about; but the deeper qualities of a person are often what form the more lasting foundations of a friendship. These qualities will be evident by the way they speak and treat others. Or in the ways they practice their faith or point others back to Jesus. Or in the ways they handle gossip, drama, or conflict. Someone who leans toward jealousy, discord, or selfish ambition might be a difficult person to form a stable friendship with. You can—and should!—still be kind, friendly, and gracious to them, but you don't have to be best friends with them or invite them into your inner circle.

The next time you are meeting a new friend, look at the fruit of her life for evidence of what is in her heart. Examine your own self and the fruit you bring into friendships. Ask God to help you grow in areas that need attention. When using the fruit of the Spirit and other godly qualities as your lens for determining next steps with friends, you don't need to worry as much about coming up with your own "red or green flags," because Scripture gives us a ready script for healthy community. Root yourself in God and He will provide the wisdom and peace you need to step into new friendships.

Friendspiration

QUALITIES OF A GOOD FRIEND

Besides the fruit of the Spirit, consider other things you might value in your friendships, keeping in mind that your definition of a good friend will change from season to season. Look at your friendship history. Make a list of a few great friends you had in previous seasons. Then write some qualities you liked about these friends. Look for similarities among the different names, and you may find trends that will surprise you regarding the type of people you enjoy spending time with.

Reflect

What's your current definition of a quality friend? How can you align your definition with the godly traits found in Scripture?

Lord, I want to be a person who produces good fruit in my life and relationships. Help me be a woman of character who points people back to You instead of someone who adds drama. Give me wisdom to nourish godly character in myself and others, and help me look for friends through this new lens. Amen.

A Desert Season

As the rain and the snow
come down from heaven,
and do not return to it
without watering the earth
and making it bud and flourish,
so that it yields seed for the sower and bread for the eater,
so is my word that goes out from my mouth:
It will not return to me empty,
but will accomplish what I desire
and achieve the purpose for which I sent it.
You will go out in joy
and be led forth in peace;
the mountains and hills
will burst into song before you,
and all the trees of the field
will clap their hands.

—ISAIAH 55:10-12

"I've tried everything *in the books to meet new friends. I've asked people to go explore new hobbies with me. I've prayed to the Lord to bring new friends into my life. I've been patient, given women second chances, and even made sacrifices to align my schedule to work with another friend's schedule. I still don't see any growth in my friendships, and I feel hopeless in my friend-making abilities."*

I've heard sentiments like this many times while coaching women in their friendships. Countless women ask what to do next after doing all the right things and still seeing zero movement toward creating a vibrant, blossoming community of friends. Many of them are tempted to call their "friendless" season a desert season—an area of their life that is dried up. Where no matter how much water they pour into their friendships, it immediately evaporates, resulting in nothing. As much as I'd love to offer these women a clear answer for what God might be doing behind the scenes, sometimes there isn't an obvious reason why.

In my early twenties, I was in a desert place with some major social dehydration. It didn't matter how much I put myself out there; I was receiving nothing in return. This experience left me raw and exposed in every area where I had hoped to find a place to belong. I watched my roommates grow close to one another and connect with others. Meanwhile, I would close myself in my room, open my computer, and watch a show alone. I felt so unlikable and envious of everyone around me who made new friendships look so easy.

During this time, I read and prayed through Isaiah 55 every single day and begged God to send rain to water my dry season of continued loneliness. I knew deep down that God champions togetherness, and I trusted His Word that says that whatever He speaks does not return to Him empty.

Eventually, my time for friendship did come, but it wasn't without hard-fought evenings of prayer and days of frustration over God's timing. But even in my hopelessness, God never gave up on me or my friendship journey.

He hasn't given up on you either, even if it feels a bit like He has. The truth is, He is championing your new friendships even when you experience disappointments or unwelcome steps backward. You might not see any growth, but God is hard at work beneath the surface transforming and renewing you, preparing you for friends who might soon be coming your way. Remember this: Being alone is not part of God's plan for you. The foundation of your friendships may not look exactly like the friendships you see around you, but that doesn't make your friendship journey any less valid. You may not experience any magical moments as everything clicks, but sometimes it takes a while to see buds sprout from the seeds you planted those many months ago.

If you are in a desert season, know that God has not abandoned you. You may feel very isolated and discouraged, but God is in that with you. Perhaps desert seasons happen so we can enjoy the blooming seasons even more. Or perhaps God is nourishing the soil of our hearts to become even richer and more life-giving for future friendships. However He is working in this season of waiting, hold on to God's Word and His promise that there will be a day when you will "go out in joy and be led forth in peace." Hold on to hope!

Reflect

From which parts of your friendship season have you been waiting for God to deliver you? How does Isaiah 55 help you hold on to hope?

Prayer

God, I feel like I have done everything I can, and I still haven't built the type of friend circle I've hoped and prayed for. I am discouraged, let down, and bordering on hopeless. It feels like everyone has a dependable friend but me. Lord, please bring someone soon who will understand me and choose to be my friend. Please help me trust that in this desert season, there is a season of joy waiting around the corner. Amen.

When Phones Disrupt Connection

Remain in me, as I also remain in you. No branch can bear fruit by itself; it must remain in the vine. Neither can you bear fruit unless you remain in me. I am the vine; you are the branches. If you remain in me and I in you, you will bear much fruit; apart from me you can do nothing.

—JOHN 15:4–5

A teacher standing on a stage holds his phone in his hand and asks the audience, "How focused on our conversation do you feel I am with my phone in my hand?" He then puts his phone down and, folding his hands in his lap, asks, "How focused do you feel I am in our conversation *now*?"

Obviously, phones were created to provide connection, and the ease with which we can call a long-distance family member or chat with an overseas friend proves this function. But unfortunately, our phones can also become crutches in socially uncomfortable situations where organic conversations used to take place. When women express their frustration to me of not being able to share conversations or make friends when they're out and about, I usually point out that, whenever we're in a waiting space, we often pull out our phones instead of talking to the person next to us. Imagine how your day might be different if you struck up a conversation while in line at the post office, chatted with the parent behind you in the school pickup line, or started an intentional discussion in the church lobby before or after a Sunday service?

This idea of intentional connection free of disruptions also applies to our relationship with God. Removing the distractions and abiding in God is what grows fruit in our lives and our relationships—not only with others, but also with Him! Trying to spend time with God while also scrolling through social media or answering work emails doesn't really allow for deep growth. It would be like carving out the time to plant your garden and then never watering it. Why even plant seeds in the first place if you aren't going to spend the time to help them grow?

I don't believe God created us to have a massive network of social connections all happening at the same time. The only one who has the capacity to be omnipresent is God. We have limits in our relationships and our attention spans. If we're going to have any chance of making genuine connections, we must put our phones or other distractions away and challenge our friends to do the same.

Whenever you start to notice a pattern of distraction in your relationships, try offering some fresh and exciting alternatives to switch things up. You could suggest an outdoor activity that would encourage everyone to disengage from the constant notification cycle and have uninterrupted conversation. You could host a no-tech dinner where everyone puts away their phone at the front door. Or you might try hosting a book club or discussion around the

intersection of technology and connection—nothing like accountability from each other! However you approach it, strive to be the person in any scenario who sparks the return of eye contact and meaningful conversation.

Reflect

What changes do you need to make to your habits in regard to your phone and your friend time?

Prayer

Lord, I know my phone is a temptation for me in social settings. It's more comfortable for me to look busy than to introduce myself to someone new. Help me to walk in this season with my eyes up, my phone out of sight, and my trust and reliance on You to give me courage to make new friends. Amen.

Friend Date

APPETIZERS AND ARTICLES

MATERIALS: snacks or a drink to share and an article you recently read or enjoyed

PREP TIME: 20 minutes

DATE TIME: 60–90 minutes

FRIENDS NEEDED: 3+

Appetizers and Articles—perfect for your intellectual, political, or pop culture friends—is a onetime commitment that could easily become a regular hangout if it turns out to be a hit. This gathering is a great way to blend new ideas and share what you've been obsessing over without the long-term commitment of a weekly Bible study or book club.

Simply invite old friends or new ones (maybe even from different social circles) to come over for appetizers and to share their favorite article from the week. It can be a political op-ed from *The New York Times* or a thought piece on women's health or faith. Encourage each person to bring a snack or drink to share and to come prepared to discuss their article and offer one question they'd like to ask the group.

With this date idea, open your minds and social appetites to feast on some good food and conversation!

Finding "Your Person"

After David had finished talking with Saul, Jonathan became one in spirit with David, and he loved him as himself.

—1 SAMUEL 18:1

In literature, there is a trope called a "meet cute": a moment when a boy and a girl have a cutesy first meeting that turns into a lasting relationship. In friendships, I like to call this same meet-cute moment a "divine appointment." In this particular friendship encounter, you immediately click, discover you like the same things, and feel safe enough to share life stories that you've previously shared with only your closest friends. These are the types of friends God brings into your life to become fast friends and soul sisters.

In adult friendships, these divine appointments are notable because they're rare. Making new friends as an adult often requires heavy lifting—a lot of coordinating back and forth and some start-stop points of connection. So when you have this instant link with someone without all the extra work, seize that friendship. It's truly a gift!

In college, I had my own divine appointment with a girl in my advisory group. After playing embarrassing games as is typical in college, she introduced herself and we realized we had a lot in common and shared similar values. After our "meet cute" of trying to climb over one another in the human pretzel game, we ended up chatting all night. Over the next four years, she became like a second home to me.

When I think of fast friends, I'm reminded of David and Jonathan in the Old Testament. Despite the fact that his dad wasn't the biggest fan of David, Jonathan took David under his wing and even made a covenant of friendship with him. He recognized a good friendship when he saw it—a friendship God arranged for both of them—and grasped on to it.

Now when I click with a friend, I try to be straightforward like Jonathan. When consistent hangouts feel impossible, I try to schedule different friend dates to make sure we still meet up regularly. I share encouraging texts to let them know how much I appreciate the budding friendship. And I try to find ways to integrate families and social circles so that we can be involved in our current communities together. Knowing these divinely appointed friendships are rare spurs me on to not take them for granted.

When you meet someone you feel like you've known your whole life, take that friendship seed from the Lord and plant it quickly. Chances are good your intuition is right, and this friendship will be blooming in no time.

Reflect

When was the last time you had an instant connection with someone? What made you know that person would become a good friend?

Prayer

Oh, this friend is so exciting! Lord, thank You for the gift of a friend that just gets me right away. Help me to cherish her and invite her into my regular friendship rhythms. And help her do the same for me! And, Lord, please work through both of us to breathe life into each other. Amen.

Friend Date

"T" PARTY

MATERIALS: "T" items for potluck, games, costumes, etc.
PREP TIME: 45–60 minutes
DATE TIME: 60–120 minutes
FRIENDS NEEDED: 4+ (also great for friends with families)

This is not your average tea party—this is a "T" party, a gathering where everything is planned to a "T" around the letter *T*.

Instruct your friends to bring a food that starts with the letter *T*, such as tacos, teriyaki chicken, tangerines, tofu, trout, tiramisu, etc. Then during the actual event, do activities that start with the letter *T*, like Twister, trampoline, trivia, or treasure hunt. If you are feeling extra creative, ask each person to dress up as a well-known figure whose name starts with the letter *T:* Thomas Edison, Taylor Swift, the Terminator, King Tut, Thomas the Tank Engine, etc.

This is friend time with a creative flair!

When You Want to Give Up

Do you not know?
Have you not heard?
The Lord is the everlasting God,
the Creator of the ends of the earth.
He will not grow tired or weary,
and his understanding no one can fathom.
He gives strength to the weary
and increases the power of the weak.
Even youths grow tired and weary,
and young men stumble and fall;
but those who hope in the Lord
will renew their strength.
They will soar on wings like eagles;
they will run and not grow weary,
they will walk and not be faint.

—ISAIAH 40:28–31

Moving to Denver at the age of twenty-two without the support of a community was an eye-opening experience. For one thing, it taught me that I really didn't know how to make friends in a new place. I started by hopping on some friend apps, but after two outings, I realized the meet-ups were much sketchier than they were helpful in supporting my search for true friends. Next, I joined a running club, but during my first run with the group, I fell behind and missed a turn somewhere. I ended up jogging back home alone. I also tried different churches and arranged some coffee dates with some of the women I met there, but none of us texted to hang out a second time. Six months after the move, I began to wonder if I could keep up the pace of constantly meeting new people without the reward of a single solid friend to show for all my effort.

If you are in a season of feeling exhausted by constantly making new connections and repeatedly telling people where you grew up and what you do for work—I get it. We all want friendships that jump straight into the fun middle instead of dancing around the edges with the interview-type questions one gets in small talk. But the truth is that meaningful friendships take time, which is something I had to learn the hard way during my first several months in Denver. In every conversation and reciprocated act of friendship, we are planting seeds that have the potential to grow into something awesome. If we don't take care of the new connections, they may never sprout into something more. Lifelong friendships don't just bloom overnight!

Thankfully, even when we get tired of trying to build community, God does not. He doesn't need to rest. His ability to move people into our path is not dependent on anything we do or don't do. And He is the One encouraging and guiding us to make the small decisions to attend the social gathering, to endure slow beginnings, and to persevere when we hit roadblocks. We may not be able to see or feel it now, but after a season of faithful planting, God will bring a season of blooming friendships.

So keep up the good work of being a friend. Nothing grows without first being planted, and if you press on in planting seeds of friendships, you will experience the joy of some of them taking root. Whenever you feel discouraged or defeated, remember this: You are a great friend. You are worthy of having great friends. And God is working all things for your good in ways you don't always understand. He doesn't ask you to jump into new friendships with the full knowledge of what will happen over the coming weeks, months, or years. Instead, He asks you to rely on Him and to be a faithful friend. With Him by your side, you can take the next small step to be faithful to the process He has invited you into.

Reflect

How can you rely on God when you feel like nothing is working out as you try to make new friends? How have you seen the hints of God working in your life to bring new friendships and connections?

Prayer

Lord, You see me in my restlessness of making new friends. I just want to be in the season where friends feel more like family than strangers. Give me the strength to keep trying and showing up. Help me endure the hard monotony of planting and bring me through to the next season of blooming friendships. Amen.

PRAYER FOR
Planting New Friendships

Do not fear, for I am with you;
do not be dismayed, for I am your God.
I will strengthen you and help you;
I will uphold you with my righteous right hand.
—ISAIAH 41:10

Lord,

You created me for connection. You formed me and molded me to desire authentic relationships with fellow believers. I know this to be true because You model real connection with the Son and the Spirit. And then You so generously invited me into that communion with You. Help me to take this generous invitation and extend it to others.

I have recently found myself needing to make new friends again, and I am discouraged. I don't even know if I have it in me to put myself out there for new friends. But I also know how lonely I've felt lately and how much I long to have a group I can call "my people." I want to step into this season with enthusiasm. I know it won't be seamless, but please give me joy in exploring new friendships.

Allow me to be open-minded toward new people I would never have expected to be real friends. Help me to be a good friend by knowing my limit and capacity—to not overpromise myself to a dozen new people without having the ability to manage all these new relationships.

And, Lord, I need so much from *You.* Fill me with courage and strength. Fill me with Your Spirit of boldness. I need You to walk beside me as I press into new relationships that demand more effort and energy in this season. I get nervous that I'll be rejected, sometimes embarrassed if I tell a joke that a new friend doesn't understand, or ashamed when friendship is hard for me. I am even afraid of my own neediness. Fill me up so that I don't put my neediness on my new friends. They don't need to complete me, because You do. That's the attitude I want to bring into this season. You are sufficient for me in this process. I can do this with You.

I'm stepping into this season completely trusting You. Help me surrender friendships that don't work out—even after I put time into them. Help me surrender the pride of believing I know better than You do about the best timeline for making a good friend. Help me surrender how I think things will go, and help me see how You grow beautiful things in my life. Help me to be obedient to do the planting.

Thank You for providing friends in the past and for how You will bless me with new friends in the future.

Amen.

Tending

Let us not become weary in doing good,
for at the proper time we will reap a
harvest if we do not give up.
—GALATIANS 6:9

GETTING REAL *with Your Friends*

He said to me, "My grace is sufficient for you, for my power is made perfect in weakness." Therefore I will boast all the more gladly about my weaknesses, so that Christ's power may rest on me. That is why, for Christ's sake, I delight in weaknesses, in insults, in hardships, in persecutions, in difficulties. For when I am weak, then I am strong.

—2 CORINTHIANS 12:9–10

Our culture has led us to believe that curating how much and what we reveal about ourselves is a necessary component to friendship. We should never share too much personal information in case a friend uses it against us and tells others. We should never be too silly or quirky, because a friend may post an embarrassing photo of us on social media. We should write and then rewrite our texts to make sure the perfect message gets across to our friends so there is no room for misinterpretation.

With these fears and the desire to steer clear of any hurt feelings embedded in our minds, we build walls and only show our friends a filtered version of ourselves. We think that if the roots of our friendships don't make it far below the surface, it won't hurt too much if we need to dig them up to plant ourselves somewhere else. But if we're concerned

about safety measures like this and protecting ourselves from any pain, how real can these friendships be?

As stress-free as they might seem, surface-level friendships don't lead to much life-giving growth—or anything else, for that matter. They may be easier to manage, but they can never compare to the friendships you tend to regularly, sow with authentic experiences, and water with care and consistency. The deeper, longer-lasting, I'll-be-there-for-you-no-matter-what-happens relationships are the ones that only develop after intentional effort is made to create safe spaces for the roots to grow deep. Tending to these friendships is indeed a risk, but it's a risk worth taking.

Something one of my best friends and I can say to each other is "I can tell you anything, and I know you won't judge me." We don't even need to say the words anymore, because we know that anything we share with each other—our fears of the day, a friendship insecurity, a funny story, an anxiety that's taking over our minds, a marriage frustration, a need for accountability, or a political critique—will be met with curiosity and kindness. A comforting and tight-knit safety exists in our friendship because we've put our embarrassing, shame-inducing things out there for each other and have always responded with "There's nothing you can do that will make me turn away from you." We're able to be open and honest with each other while also receiving those honest confessions with appropriate amounts of prayer, pep talks, and iced teas from Starbucks. But it has taken a lot of trust, work, and time to get to that point.

If we don't want shallow friendships, we need to cultivate an atmosphere of vulnerability and safety. I know it's not easy. Being vulnerable is like handing a precious and fragile family heirloom to someone else and trusting that person to take care of it as much as you have. In return, you want to be a *safe* person—a trusted friend who can carry sensitive information about others and communicate, "Look, I've seen your ugly stuff, and I *still* won't turn away from you."

I know I am tending to the right friendships when I don't have to filter my stories or my thoughts for my friends to accept me. Of course, we should practice a healthy balance of vulnerability and boundaries, because obviously we shouldn't tell everything to every person we meet. But having the wisdom to know what and when and with whom to share isn't the same as curating a self that we think people will like or accept. No matter how much or how little you share, your goal should be to present a genuine version of you so you can create a genuine bond with others.

The more we get real with each other, the more we can love each other. It's friendship math that makes sense! It's difficult to care for people when we only see half of them. Letting your friends love you requires showing them all sides of yourself—your silliness, your bravery, your stressors, and your irrational fears. This is probably why God's love feels so unique, since He knows everything about you and still calls you friend.

As an added benefit, practicing honesty will also model the type of honesty you expect *from* your friends. Yes, it's hard to go first, but you might be surprised by how others receive your vulnerability. Sometimes my most stilted new-friend conversations find their groove when I finally share something I've been worried about. Sharing our true selves reminds every friend that we are all more alike than different.

Reflect

Do you struggle with letting people know the real you? What parts of yourself are harder to share? How have you experienced the joy of being authentic with others?

Prayer

Lord, I am anxious to let my friends know the real me. What if they don't like me? What if they realize—when the shield is down—that I am seriously imperfect with glaring flaws, and they don't want to be my friend anymore? Lord, give me courage to be me and to release my need to be seen as perfect. Provide safe friends who will still love me when I am my true self. Amen.

Ending the Cynicism Cycle

Do not let any unwholesome talk come out of your mouths, but only what is helpful for building others up according to their needs, that it may benefit those who listen.
—EPHESIANS 4:29

Have you ever had a friend who connects to you primarily by complaining about other people? Have you ever done that? It can certainly be tempting to label a person or group as "other," especially if doing so makes you feel closer to someone else. You might complain about a boss or co-worker who has made your job more difficult, a leader at church who always schedules events at inconvenient times, or a mutual friend who has been acting weird or distant ever since she got into a serious relationship. These types of conversations can feel gratifying since they allow you to air all your inner negative thoughts and find someone who will validate your feelings. However, basing friendships on this kind of negative talk can be unhealthy and even dangerous in the long run.

As you tend to the friendships in your life, notice which ones are based more on tearing others down versus building others up. Pay attention to the friendships and situations in which you tend to lean more toward the negative and take note of which friends seem to increase that temptation. This isn't to say that you should never discuss hard or frustrating things with friends, but if criticism makes up 90 percent of what you talk about, then you might want to take a step back and reevaluate whether your conversation is actually gossiping.

I was in a young Christian mom circle in which most of our time was spent sharing the complaints about confusing pediatric advice, unhelpful partners, or moms who made us feel judged for having different parenting styles. After a couple of months, I couldn't pinpoint exactly what I was feeling about the group. It took another mom standing up to everyone and confronting us with how we were using our words for me to realize we were in a cycle of negativity. The courageous mom reminded us that no matter what difficulties we might be facing in motherhood, we could still use our words to champion the good and true things in our lives. It was a wake-up call.

Pulling a friendship away from a complaining habit is not easy, but replacing bad practices with healthy ones rarely is. If you find yourself struggling in this area, think about the garden you are tending to—whatever you sow, you reap. If you don't want to be the subject of someone else's gossip, don't spread your own. If you don't enjoy being in the company of a critical spirit, then don't feed the monster. If negativity has become a pattern in your friend group, start intentionally spreading positivity. Even if someone keeps coming to you with problems and issues, receive their complaint with grace and respond with prayer and compassion. Encourage your friends with God's truth, and watch your friendships shift from criticisms to care. Share words that give life!

Reflect

With which friends are you tempted to spend most of your time complaining and criticizing others? How can you encourage your friends to reach for truth and grace instead of constant criticism?

Prayer

Lord, I know I can be critical and that I often try to garner sympathy by bringing friends into my issues with others to affirm my feelings. I confess that this cycle of negativity has not been a healthy space for my friendships, and I want us to be a community of friends who speak kindly, graciously, and truthfully. Restore joy to our conversations and give us the discipline to be considerate with our words. Amen.

Friend Date

TRADE SWAP

MATERIALS: meeting space (a home, park, coffee shop, or another gathering place); items to trade (clothing, jewelry, knick-knacks, etc.)

PREP TIME: 20–30 minutes

DATE TIME: 1–2 hours

FRIENDS NEEDED: 4+

Whether your friend group is into reading and listening to records, cookware and coffee mugs, or jewelry or gym accessories, the trade swap offers the perfect opportunity to get together and share your interests. Simply set a date, choose a location, and tell every friend you invite to bring an item or two to be traded. The rule is that guests can swap only the number of items they bring. (For example, if someone brings a sweater and a book, they can go home with two items brought by someone else.) As guests arrive, invite them to place their items on a table and then mingle to allow time for latecomers. At a designated time, announce that the table is open for trading and tell your friends to walk around and select the used item they'd like to take home.

Keep the event logistics simple by offering lemonade and store-bought cookies or by hosting your trade swap at a local coffee shop or brewery where guests can purchase their own food and drinks.

By the end of the event, you might gain a new item for yourself as well as a new friend to connect with!

Carry Each Other's Burdens

Carry each other's burdens, and in this way you will fulfill the law of Christ.

—GALATIANS 6:2

I sit down to meet my friend for coffee—a typical Saturday morning catch-up. We laugh, we share some work frustrations, but I keep the conversation light. I want my friend to think I am relatable but not a total disaster (as in my hair is in an unwashed bun, but I still made *some* effort to put on real pants and earrings). So I make sure to share just enough to create a connection, but not enough to let her see all the anxieties I carry.

I held up this façade of being a shinier version of myself for most of my life until one inevitable day when I couldn't handle my hard things on my own. I had been battling depression for a few months during college, but I had never told anyone. I would cry in class, I would cry while reading a book, and I would cry while running. There was just a lot of sadness I couldn't control. But none of my friends noticed, because I kept plastering on a smile and sharing about how *great* my faith was.

Unfortunately, my inability to tell my friends about my depression only made me feel lonelier. When I finally shared the truth with some close friends, they felt like I had been dishonest with them for not speaking up and sharing what was really going on in my life. Were we even friends if I couldn't share the fullness of my emotions with them?

In our world today, being "needy" holds a ton of negative connotations. We respect and admire independence while we reject and criticize neediness. Yet being so focused on independence also separates us from others. Being a good friend is difficult when we don't know what is going on beneath the surface of each other's lives. Still, for some reason, we often don't want people to know that we have physical, emotional, and spiritual needs. We want them to believe we're carefree. But real friendships aren't based on our ability to put on a perfect face. So how can we strive to be honest, to express our needs when they come up, and to have compassion for one another's circumstances?

The author of Galatians charged us to serve one another by carrying each other's burdens (Galatians 6:2). We might think we need friends who love us for our perkiness and positivity, but really, we need friends who love us despite our difficulties and issues. As Christ bears with us in our weaknesses, we are also to bear the weaknesses of others. Not to take *on* the burden and carry it ourselves, but to carry it *to* God in prayer on behalf of our friends.

Life demands a lot, but God gifted us with friends who want to help. In return, we can open the door for mutual sharing and serving. We can do hard things together.

Reflect

Why is it so difficult to share your needs with your friends? Who is one person you could talk to today about the real worries, anxieties, or challenges going on in your life?

Prayer

Lord, I am so nervous to show my friends the not-so-pretty side to my life. I want to be seen and known, but I'm also deeply afraid to be seen and known. Help me to recognize which trusted friends I can share my life's deepest struggles with, knowing they will have compassion for me. Help us carry each other's burdens to You and show Your love to one another. Amen.

Friend Date

CHARCUTERIE AND CHARADES

MATERIALS: several slips or scraps of paper (2–3 per person), pens or pencils, a bowl, and charcuterie fixings

PREP TIME: 5–10 minutes **DATE TIME:** 1–2 hours

FRIENDS NEEDED: 5+

This friend date is great for new or old friends and also perfect for families. To add something extra to the gathering with very little effort, create a charcuterie board and serve your favorite drinks with it. (My kids have been into *charfruiteries* lately—a board with only fruit. Huge hit!) Make it budget-friendly by having each guest bring an item for the charcuterie board so you're not providing all the refreshments yourself.

Once everyone arrives, gather in a circle and give each guest two to three scraps of paper. Instruct them to write down a person, place, or thing on each piece (writing the names of celebrities, books, or movies can be fun too).* Throw all the papers into a bowl. After breaking into two teams and choosing team names (don't miss this step!), pass the bowl around the circle and have each guest choose a paper and act out what is written on it. You can let each person draw one piece of paper, or you can set a timer for 30–40 seconds and see how many words each person can get through. Variations besides charades include a catchphrase round (the person holding the bowl has to describe what is written on each piece of paper without saying any of the words on the paper) and a password round (the person holding the bowl can only say one word to describe what is written on the paper). After each round, tally up how many correct guesses each team made.

Enjoy an hour or so of fun!

* If there are kiddos in your group, consider printing off some pictures so that non-readers can participate as well.

Quality over Quantity

Suppose one of you wants to build a tower. Won't you first sit down and estimate the cost to see if you have enough money to complete it? For if you lay the foundation and are not able to finish it, everyone who sees it will ridicule you, saying, "This person began to build and wasn't able to finish."

—LUKE 14:28–30

A friend of mine recently decided to start a garden in her backyard. Because she wanted a good crop and lots of blooms, she planted every vegetable she could make space for. But as the sprouts began to emerge from the dirt, she realized that only some of the vegetables were growing. Many others withered quickly or failed to take root at all. The discouragement she felt over the failed veggies almost overcame the joy she experienced over the ones that had grown, but the whole ordeal taught her an important lesson. The following year, she decided she'd focus on only one or two vegetables instead of ten.

During any "tending" season of friendship, when our enthusiasm for new friends is higher than usual, we can easily become distracted by the allure of more—just as my friend did with her vegetable garden. After all, filling our social calendar with friend dates and increasing our contact list is fun. But as exciting as it is to be out of the desert season and into a period of growth, we must also recognize our limits and avoid the temptation to stretch ourselves too thin. We don't want to overcommit to a bunch of new friends only to end up canceling several hangouts when we realize we don't have the time or energy to keep our promises to all of them.

And just as my friend learned with her garden, we should not get disappointed or discouraged if our new friendships don't all work out in the same way or at the same pace. Instead, we should focus on the joy we feel over the friendships that *do* succeed. We're not going to score a one hundred in every friendship, and that's okay.

In my twenties, many of my birthday parties involved guest lists with dozens of friends, but as time and life went on, my guest lists became smaller. So much so that I began to wonder if something was wrong with me. Was I not valuing my friends the way I used to? Was I failing in my ability to keep up with several friends at once? Was I losing some of my friendship magic? Thankfully, when I took a closer look at the friends who were still gathering to celebrate with me, I realized that the shorter guest list had nothing to do with the depth of my connection to each person. If anything, my relationships were deeper! In other words, investing in *fewer* friends allowed me to cultivate *deeper quality* friendships.

Every relationship comes with challenges—and the temptation to spread ourselves too thinly is one of them. As Jesus warned us in Luke, "If you lay the foundation and are not able to finish it, everyone who sees it will ridicule you." Put another way, we should try to build a circle of friendships we can see all the way through. To weigh our limitations and availability before promising to do more for our friends. To cultivate quality over quantity.

Reflect

Are you ever tempted to add more to your relational bank? If so, how can you discern which friendships you should tend to most right now?

Prayer

Lord, You have blessed me with so many friends in this season. I am so excited to get to know new people in my community, but I need help setting boundaries with my time and resources so I don't overextend myself. I don't want to be spread so thinly that I am incapable of tending to any friendships at all. Instead, help me narrow down where I can focus my energy so I can be an even better friend. Amen.

When Good Friendships Get Bumpy

[Love] always protects, always trusts, always hopes, always perseveres.
—1 CORINTHIANS 13:7

You've done it! You've finally hit it off with an awesome new friend. Perhaps the two of you have been attending the same weekly workout class, or maybe you've been trying out a new restaurant together every week or so. Whatever the basis of your friendship, the relationship has been marked by consistency, reciprocity, and mutual enjoyment of each other.

But then something happens—a subtle shift—and you notice the blissful "honeymoon phase" starting to wear off. Perhaps aligning your calendars has become more difficult. Or maybe you had your first disagreement on faith or politics. Or one of you skipped over some text responses. Suddenly, you're not sure if this is a friendship that is going to last.

The good thing about friendships in today's culture is that we can easily connect with new people in so many ways, both online and off. The downside of this "friendship at our fingertips" is that walking away from a friendship when it gets difficult is just as easy. And too often, we listen to the lie that "when a friendship hits a bump in the road, you should abandon it." But if we make a habit of ghosting our friends or creating distance when the going gets tough, we will end up stuck on a Ferris wheel of start-stop friendships—forever going round and round in a pattern of sameness without ever reaching the depth of the real relationships we truly crave.

The world often tells us that love and healthy friendships can only be found with people who make us feel good all the time, who affirm our thoughts and actions, and who make our lives feel like a perfect Saturday morning every time we are together. After all, loving those who support us, match our vibe, and serve our needs is easy. But true friendship—friendship that can withstand time, trials, and differences—can't be based on these traits alone.

In 1 Corinthians, Paul reminded us that true love protects, trusts, hopes, and perseveres in *all* things. This definition—God's definition—is vastly different from the world's definition. When we practice loving like God does, we will protect and fight for our friendships even when our friends annoy or irritate us. We will hope for the best in our friends and look for their good qualities instead of their faults. We will persevere to maintain our strong bonds even when our friendships aren't as shiny or easy as they were at the beginning. In other words, if we want to pursue meaningful friendships, we need to meaningfully practice and live out God's love.

One helpful practice I have is scheduling my friend dates way in advance. Instead of allowing busyness to be a hurdle in connecting, I make plans one or two months out. My husband does this too. He has a monthly lunch date scheduled with a bud, on repeat in both of their calendars.

Each month, they simply check in to make sure the date still works. But it's always on the schedule.

People may think that planning friend dates like it's a side hustle makes friendship feel less organic. But really, it shows our friends that, despite how difficult finding time together may be, we want to thoughtfully plan it out.

So rather than becoming discouraged when the honeymoon phase of your friendship ends, see it as an opportunity to bring your friendship to a deeper level. Face any hurdles or challenges with fierce perseverance and test your own character by preparing for any sacrifices that may have to be made. As you and your friend grow together, remember that though the honeymoon phase may be "all fun all the time," what comes after plants the true seeds of genuine and lasting connection.

Friendspiration

AFTER THE HONEYMOON PHASE

Consistency is everything in a budding friendship—especially in ones where you click so well. Don't be embarrassed to eagerly pursue this friend. Tell her you want to spend more time together. Adjust invitations to fit her into your other social circles. Get your kids to sign up for the same soccer league so you can chat on the sidelines. Ask your spouses to agree to a monthly game night. If you've found this unique friend in this season, go all in!

Reflect

How has a friend stuck by you even when your friendship got a little rocky? How have you noticed your friendships forming stronger roots after the honeymoon phase ends?

Prayer

Lord, You have blessed me with friendships that are fun and easygoing, but I understand that every moment won't be marked by mountaintop highs. When the friendships require a little sacrifice or more effort on my part, give me the heart to persevere. Grow good fruit in these friendships through our faithfulness to each other. Amen.

When Friendship Requires Sacrifice

Greater love has no one than this: to lay down one's life for one's friends.

—JOHN 15:13

Several years ago, when one of my friends was preparing to leave for college, I found out he was low on cash for gas money and textbooks. While praying for this friend one evening, an idea popped into my head: *What if I held a garage sale and raised the money my friend needed?* It seemed like quite the undertaking for one person, but after asking my mom about it and praying over the idea some more, I decided to do it. Moreover, I made my plans in secret so my friend would be less likely to refuse the help.

In preparation, I went through my closet and unearthed old homecoming dresses, shoes, bags, and books that I could sacrifice for the cause. Because my cousin lived in a more high-traffic part of town, she kindly allowed me to use her front yard and overwhelm her garage with tables and items for sale. On the very first day—even though I had practically zero garage sale experience—the Lord blessed the efforts, and we sold almost everything. In total, we raised eight hundred dollars!

The garage sale regulars told me this level of success was unheard of, but I knew it was God's doing. He was rewarding my obedience to Him. When I handed the money over to my friend with no strings attached and watched his shocked reaction to the generosity of God's provision, I knew giving up my stuff had been completely worth it.

Making sacrifices for our friends is not about if but when, since there will come a time in every relationship when a friend will need your support. The sacrifice may not look like an entire garage sale of your personal items, but it could involve you driving a friend to the airport late at night, agreeing to cat-sit so a friend can enjoy their family vacation, or joining an activity or outing that wouldn't normally be your first choice. Sacrifices don't have to be huge or dramatic to mean something. Any selfless act or gift that involves us setting aside our own wants, wishes, or way shows our friends that we care about them and also allows us to follow in Jesus's footsteps.

Jesus explained that a friend is one who lays down his life for his friends. He put those words into action when He died on the cross for all of us in the ultimate act of love. Even though we likely won't be called upon to die for any of our friends, Jesus does invite us into the smaller death of dying to self. And when we heed this call to put aside our own wants for the sake of others, we will be instilling our friendships with new depths of love.

So the next time an opportunity arises for you to sacrifice some of your personal comforts in order to better serve a friend, seize it as a chance to live out Jesus's sacrificial love. May the world know us by our love for each other, as John wrote in his first letter: "No one has ever seen God; but if we love one another, God lives in us and his love is made complete in us" (1 John 4:12).

Reflect

What are some of your most difficult comforts to give up? How might God be calling you to serve your friends out of sacrificial love?

Prayer

Lord, Your kindness toward me is unmatched. You showed me and the rest of the world the greatest act of friendship when You laid down Your life for us. Help me take an ounce of that passion and put it toward my friendships. I want to care for and serve my friends even when it feels uncomfortable or inconvenient. Help me to step out of my own selfish tendencies or fears of giving myself away to step into love instead. Amen.

Friendspiration

ASKING FOR HELP

How do we balance asking our friends for help without over-asking?

This may come as a surprise, but asking friends to help out is not as big a deal as you may have built it up to be. Everyone secretly wants a role in and a reason for supporting their friends. Being specific about how you need help can clarify the ways a friend can be there for you. When a friend offers help, say yes; don't be too timid to ask for the support you need.

We also need to be okay when a friend can't help out. That doesn't mean they don't love us. Maybe it just means they aren't the type of friend we see in sitcoms, where nobody ever seems to be working or folding laundry or doing all the other activities a normal person is required to do. Pressing for help when you know a friend can't give it is when lines can be crossed. You have to trust that when you need help with something, your friend knows their own capacity for whether they are able to say yes.

When a Friendship Is One-Sided

**We know and rely on the love God has for us.
God is love. Whoever lives in love
lives in God, and God in them.**
—1 JOHN 4:16

If I just *invite her over for dinner, then maybe she'll invite me over for dinner soon.*

Okay, she hasn't extended an invitation to dinner, and it's been six months. Maybe if I offer to take her kids on a fun playdate, then she'll include me in her next girls' night?

Well, that was chaotic, but maybe she'll notice how much I cared for her kids and she'll be the one to initiate a walk around the neighborhood . . .

This one-sided friendship with my neighbor (let's call her Katherine) went on and on for two years. I was desperate to be her friend. She was amazing, our kids were the same age, and she was a fellow Christian whom I could walk alongside as we both navigated marriage and motherhood. But after months of my initiating dates and her always having an excuse for why her schedule didn't align with mine, I finally gave up my dream of ever being her best friend . . . or even friends at all.

Maybe you have experienced a one-sided friendship just like this. Perhaps you played a similar game, hoping that if you just changed this one thing about yourself or went that extra mile, then that friend would finally reciprocate your efforts. But the truth is that some friendships will lead to dead ends. You could move the world for them only for them to continue ignoring their side of the relationship.

It wasn't until a faithful friend had a hard conversation with me about my hurt from the friendship with that neighbor that I was able to step outside my situation and see the friendship for what it really was: transactional. A transactional friendship isn't true friendship since it doesn't involve mutual respect and kindness. As much as you may like a person, a transactional friendship with someone may cause more pain than good simply because it will always leave you on edge, wondering if you'll ever do enough to keep the other person satisfied.

Thankfully, a relationship with God is never transactional and will never be one-sided. He loves you for *you* and will always be close to listen to you, comfort you, and challenge you. He did not create you to chase after people who show little to no interest in spending time with you. So, if you've been tiring yourself out with a one-sided friendship, take a step back and ask yourself if you might be searching for acceptance in an unforgiving environment.

Admittedly, being in a transactional friendship will result in a wound that takes time to heal. You may have to rewrite all the "Maybe I did too much of this . . ." and "If only I had said that . . ." with the one truth you do have: At the end of the day, God is still with you and can carry your pain for you. And when you're ready, let that friendship go and turn toward relationships that have the potential to be more mutual. Grieving what could have been with that one-sided friend is okay, but don't let yourself get stuck in a dead-end relationship when God might be waiting for you to accept something even better.

Friendspiration

CHOOSING HONESTY

If you're the one who's been holding a friend at a distance, you may need to do the brave thing and either apologize and repair the relationship or tell her you're no longer as deeply invested and need to take a step back. In either case, let her know what you've enjoyed about your friendship or the season you shared together. If you are planning to step away, bless her by saying you hope she finds other friends that will match the level of commitment you haven't been able to give. These kinds of conversations are never easy, but if done well and with kindness and clarity, you can free others from any anxiety or confusion they might be feeling instead of faking it for the sake of avoiding hurt feelings.

Reflect

How have you dealt with one-sided friendships in the past? If you're in one now, what can you do either to encourage equal effort on the other person's side or to protect your own boundaries?

Prayer

Lord, I have been stuck in one-sided friendships before and may be in one even now. I need Your love to carry me through my next steps of how to approach this friend or end the friendship. Heal the wounds I've felt through this experience and help me not to lose confidence in my value as a good friend, even if others don't always appreciate it. Amen.

Giving Grace

Bear with each other and forgive one another if any of you has a grievance against someone. Forgive as the Lord forgave you.
—COLOSSIANS 3:13

When one of my close friends had her first baby, she stopped returning my texts. As a mother of two myself, I remembered what it was like having a newborn, but I still felt hurt. Surely my friend could muster up the energy to talk to *her best friend,* right? I wanted to be included in the details of this new part of her life, and I felt a bit left out.

As you read this, you might be tempted to judge me or say something like, *Relax, Bailey, she'll get to you when she gets to you. She just had a baby, for crying out loud!* Believe me, I get it. I *knew* all of that in my head, but for some reason, that knowledge didn't stop my heart from experiencing hurt. Maybe you can relate.

No matter how tight you and your friends are (or maybe even *because* of how tight you are), you will disappoint your friends and they will disappoint you. Often, there will be a perfectly good reason for the disappointment, whether because of miscommunication, a bad mood, a simple mistake, or something else. But when we fail to address the issue head-on and instead stew about it internally, we often can create an unnecessary conflict that might even work its way into the heart of our friendships.

Did my friend purposely hurt my feelings, or did she just miss the memo?

Is she really missing my birthday because of a work thing, or does she just not want to come?

Is she quieter today because she's not feeling well, or is she mad at me for something I did?

The problem with overanalyzing our friendship interactions is that doing so often results in our taking on unhealthy self-esteem issues and believing untrue things about ourselves and our friends. Sometimes we might even get saucy with our friends in ways that feel totally unprompted and unexpected to them, simply because we're holding on to false beliefs about them or the friendship in general. And in worst-case scenarios, our bad attitudes can spark unnecessary conflicts.

In Colossians, Paul urged believers to bear with each other and forgive one another. In other words, we should be patient with each other and quick to forgive, whether the slight was intentional or only perceived. This isn't to say that our friends are necessarily "sinning" when they disappoint us or act in a way contrary to what we would prefer. In many cases, the fault is entirely with us having a certain expectation—whether verbalized or not—that then leads to a disappointment. But no matter what the situation is, extending love despite hurt feelings and offering grace instead of frustration can go a long way in soothing any injuries and shoring up our own insecurities. After all, isn't that what Jesus does for us whenever we mess up?

Going back to those earlier statements, let's reimagine them from a perspective of grace instead of hurt and see how the narrative changes:

My friend did hurt my feelings with what she said, but I know her and know she would never hurt me on purpose. I might give her some time, and then I'll ask her in a loving and nonconfrontational way if we can talk about what happened.

I hate that my bestie is missing my birthday, but I know she loves me. Maybe I'll ask if the two of us can do something to celebrate later.

My friend is quieter today, but instead of worrying about it and coming up with all sorts of made-up possibilities of what I might have done, I should just ask her if she's okay and if there's anything I've done to upset her.

Having compassion for others in the same way we would want compassion extended to us can really help us show grace to our friends. And instead of jumping to wrong conclusions or imagined scenarios, we should also reach first for truth and understanding through communication.

Four weeks after my friend had her baby, she reached out to tell me that she missed me and would love for me to come see her soon. Her reminder of how much our friendship meant to her made me feel so silly for thinking she was being a bad friend. It taught me a real lesson in practicing grace and clarity in all my friendships.

Reflect

How can you practice grace and healthy communication when your friends do something that disappoints you?

Prayer

Lord, I know my friends are not perfect and that their friendship with me is not the center of their world, but sometimes I feel forgotten or intentionally left out. Help me battle against negative thoughts and give me the courage to have honest conversations with my friends when they intentionally or unintentionally hurt my feelings. Help me to forgive when it's needed and to always extend grace. Amen.

Friend Date

A MINI-RETREAT

MATERIALS: snacks or meal ingredients, spa items, journaling supplies

PREP TIME: 60 minutes **DATE TIME:** 4–6 hours

FRIENDS NEEDED: 1–6

Busier schedules can be worked around with short or easy-to-plan friend dates, but when you find opportunities for longer visits, take them. A mini-retreat with friends offers a great chance to escape the busyness of the season and rest and recharge together.

Since a retreat requires a greater amount of time, try to plan everything in advance, including a few different activity options in case you need to pivot last minute due to weather or cancellations. If you have kids, make sure you figure out childcare in advance too, for you and your friends.

One simpler type of retreat could include hosting your friends at your home for a meal you prepare together. You can plan the menu and assign each person to bring a specific item to contribute. Your time together can then be spent cooking or baking. If you make extra, you can even send each friend home with a takeaway box after you enjoy the meal together.

If you have extra time after your meal, you could plan some kind of spa element, like face masks or pedicures. If you and your friends have the funds and ability to go all out, schedule a massage therapist to come and give twenty-minute massages to everyone.

Finally, consider building some silence into a portion of your day to allow you and your friends time to read, do a relaxing craft, or journal. While you munch on the yummy meal you made together and enjoy each other's conversation, you can relax with the knowledge that you don't have to brainstorm dinner because it's already prepped.

A friend-filled Saturday like this can be difficult to carve out of everyone's schedules, but it's worth it for the intentional time to rest and be together.

MAINTAINING FRIENDSHIPS *Across Faith Backgrounds*

In the same way, let your light shine before others, that they may see your good deeds and glorify your Father in heaven.

—MATTHEW 5:16

Navigating relationships with friends who don't share your same faith or values can be tricky at best and challenging at worst. As close as you might be, you may still feel "other" from them, like an outsider who doesn't always share the same experiences or even speak the same language. In more dramatic situations, you may worry that you'll come across as judgy or prudish when you turn down an invitation because it goes against your beliefs. What if your friends stop inviting you to spend time with them? What if you make them think all Christians are stuck up or narrow-minded?

When Jesus was on earth, He didn't do the predictable thing of spending all His time with the religious leaders. One would think those would have been His people. That He would have chatted Old Testament Scripture with God's people all day, led prayer circles, and only broken bread with "spiritual" people on the Sabbath. Instead, He spent most of His time with people the religious crowd wouldn't have expected (or approved of): the "sinners" like tax collectors, lepers, outcasts, women, and even children—none of whom knew the Old Testament prophecies by heart. In fact, Jesus often spoke out *against* the religious leaders.

While we should certainly maintain close communion with God and other believers, we should also pay attention to Jesus's example of being a welcoming presence to all. We shouldn't be afraid of spending time with people of other faiths or being a little unlike our non-Christian friends. After all, our "otherness" might be the exact thing that draws these friends to us. So instead of being like the religious leaders of Jesus's time, who rejected those who didn't live their faith according to "their law," we should aim to be more like Jesus, who stopped to greet and spend time with those who were often overlooked.

If you're currently experiencing doubts or concerns about your friendships with people who don't share your faith, consider this: You may be the only person your friends feel safe to talk to because you've proven yourself to be compassionate and trustworthy. You may be the only person they have shared a deep struggle with because they know you pray for them. You may be the only light in their lives.

So even if you're feeling like the odd one out, remember that God may be using you and working through you in the lives of your non-believing friends. These beloved friends of yours are also beloved to God, created by Him, and made in His image. And who knows? God may have put them in your life so that you could make Him known to them.

Reflect

What aspects of your friendships with people who don't share your faith do you struggle with the most? In what ways can you share the love of God with these friends, and how can you remember to pray for them more consistently?

Prayer

Lord, I often feel set apart from my friends who do not share the same faith as me. I want to be involved and included in these communities, but I also want to be faithful to my beliefs. Help me to emulate Your caring character to every person and to be a welcoming presence to all I meet. You are a light in my life! Shine through me to others. Amen.

PRAYER FOR *a Struggling Friend*

Praise be to the God and Father of our Lord Jesus Christ, the Father of compassion and the God of all comfort, who comforts us in all our troubles, so that we can comfort those in any trouble with the comfort we ourselves receive from God. For just as we share abundantly in the sufferings of Christ, so also our comfort abounds through Christ.

—2 CORINTHIANS 1:3–5

Lord,

You are the great Comforter. Right now I have a friend who is walking through some hard things, and I do not know how to comfort her. I don't have the right words, I don't know how to care for her, and I certainly don't know how to fix her broken heart. Only You can provide what I am lacking as a friend in this situation and what my friend is needing in her spirit.

My friend has been so low lately, and I feel lost in trying to care for her. I feel pressure to have all the answers, even though I know I don't have to fix her situation because You hold all things together. I know You are watching over her, and You won't let one thing slip from Your eye. Yet I still want to be Your hands and feet to her and a support to her in her time of need.

Help me to . . .

- be a comfort in ways that are comforting to her,
- know when to bring a meal or a listening ear,
- discern when it's the right time to tell her, "God is with you,"
- serve her in ways that don't feel too overwhelming,
- understand my own capacity and know when to say, "I can't be there for you today,"
- gather our friend group to rally around her in prayer,
- have patience when her grieving lasts longer than she ever expected,
- show grace when she cancels last minute because showing up feels too raw,
- give tough love when she needs to hear that her thoughts are not based in truth,
- remember to text her thoughtful encouragement,
- bring bits of sunshine back into her week,
- host a friend night to show her that she still has people who care about her,
- support her by cleaning up around the house while she takes a moment to herself,
- cry with her because we both feel the sadness she's experiencing,

- go with her to do the hard thing she hasn't brought herself to do yet,
- tell her all the things I love about her even when she feels unlovable,
- fight back against the lies she believes about herself,
- follow through when I tell her I will be a consistent friend in this season, and
- hold faith for her when she has stopped believing You will come through for her.

Lord, there are so many ways to serve my friend as she walks through this hard thing. Help me to know the next right thing to do. Even though I want to see her restored back to the place she was before, allow me to see her through her trying season and find her not only restored but also brought into a new version of herself that is able to hold both joy and pain at the same time.

God, You are in control of her situation. Bring peace. Bring healing. Bring Your joy back into her life.

Amen.

Pruning

I am the true vine, and my Father is the gardener. He cuts off every branch in me that bears no fruit, while every branch that does bear fruit he prunes so that it will be even more fruitful.

—JOHN 15:1–2

Tough Conversations

As iron sharpens iron,
so one person sharpens another.
—PROVERBS 27:17

Working up the courage to tell a friend they have hurt you is one of the biggest hurdles in a friendship. Saying what you feel can be uncomfortable because you don't want it to be interpreted the wrong way and threaten the peace in the relationship. There are plenty of situations that you can let slide, but there are other times when you *know* you need to say something.

Perhaps one of your friends has hurt your feelings, but you're nervous about how she'll react if you tell her. Or perhaps you have a friend who has stopped coming to Bible study and you aren't sure how to address the lack of care since you kind of feel that she has ghosted the group. Or you notice weird tension between you and a friend after a joke you made—she seems to be ignoring you when you try to make eye contact from across the table, and you know it's on you to bring it up.

In an ideal world, these conflicts and messy feelings would just disappear, and the friendship could miraculously go back to the way it was before anything happened. I'd certainly like to wave a wand and do away with all tough conversations,

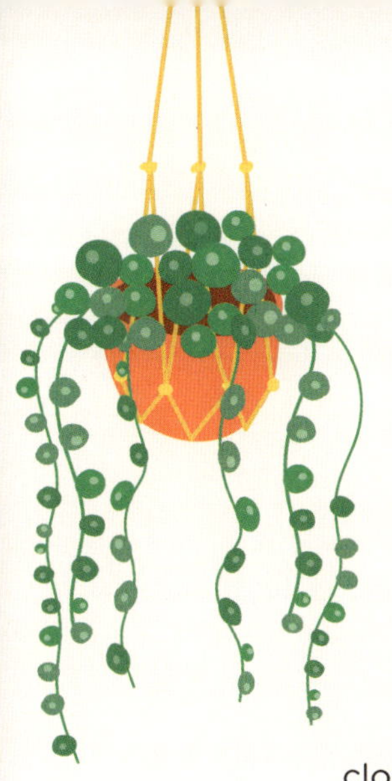

but the Lord intended for us to correct and challenge each other while pointing to Jesus's love and forgiveness. And when the conversation is approached thoughtfully, correction can be extremely helpful and even life-giving. After all, how are we to grow if the people closest to us—the ones who have seen and lived all our different seasons—ignore our potentially harmful or dangerous tendencies instead of guiding us back to truth?

For example, if the continued behavior of a close friend is hurting you, consider pulling that friend aside and speaking with her directly (see Matthew 18:15).

If you see a friend doing something wrong, talk to her about it and restore her to her faith with gentleness (see Galatians 6:1).

When a friend is wrestling with her faith or having doubts about God's Word, use your words to encourage her (see 1 Thessalonians 5:14).

When two iron knives are scraped together, they become sharper, giving them the best chance to do what they are meant to do. In the same way, God has given us friends to sharpen us and for us to sharpen them so that we can all do what He has planned for us to do. The ways you and your friends speak to and show up for each other really make a difference. Your words can lift friends out of a bad day, remind them of what is true and right, and shape their character.

As much as I want cozy friendships that never have to address uncomfortable tensions, a friendship that is "faking fine" isn't going to lead to growth. So instead of worrying about what your friends will think if you start up a hard conversation, maybe you should consider what will happen if you never confront anything at all. God has entrusted us with each other and given us the influence in one another's lives to speak boldly *and* gently as ambassadors of God's Word for "teaching, rebuking, correcting and training in righteousness" (2 Timothy 3:16). What we do as ambassadors is up to us.

Friendspiration

HANDLING CONFLICT

Tough conversations take a lot of courage. Practice writing out what you'd like to say before you meet with your friend, so you can process your thoughts in a non-pressure environment. Then be clear with your friend beforehand on why you are getting together. If she goes into the conversation believing it is only a casual catch-up, your words will catch her off guard, and she will be more likely to be defensive. Finally, pray!

Reflect

In which friendships might you need to have a tough conversation? What will your first action step be?

Lord, I am nervous and afraid that what I might need to say will cause more hurt in the friendship. I love this friend and so I feel led to say something, but I need Your courage and Your words to speak through me. Help me to speak kindly and graciously to my friend. Let my friends know that I care enough about them to have these tough conversations. Amen.

WHEN A FRIEND Cancels at the Last Minute

Whoever would foster love covers over an offense, but whoever repeats the matter separates close friends.

—PROVERBS 17:9

My husband was hosting a football watch party but quickly became discouraged when he received texts throughout the day from some of the guys who were canceling on him at the last minute. He had gone above and beyond a month in advance to set a date that would work for the majority of his friends, and he was understandably frustrated.

I was helping prepare snacks in the kitchen when he came in after calling his co-host, and with a loud sigh he asked, "How do you do this? Friends cancel on you all the time, and now I know it doesn't feel good. I'm so frustrated. I just want to give up and cancel the whole thing."

If you're human and have ever had someone cancel on you, you get it. It feels like a rejection. You put in the effort and planning, only for someone to cancel because *they* are tired. All the hard work you did feels unnoticed and underappreciated.

When friends cancel at the last minute, it communicates a lot more than someone having an unpredictable schedule. It can communicate:

> "You're not a priority to me."
>
> "Your time and effort are not valuable to me."
>
> "I have something better to do than spending time with you."
>
> "You can't count on or trust me."

What may seem like a small decision for them can feel like a huge insult for you as the host.

I have planned many events in which I expected fifteen people to show up . . . only for five to come. It basically meant there was a pizza for each person! So, when Tim's friends bailed on him, I was able to explain, "This is one of the burdens of hosting. You plan, you prep, you pray, and people still might not feel up to coming. But you do it anyway. You do it for the people that *do* come. You do it for your own soul that is hungry for connection. And you have the courage to do it again, because you believe in giving people second chances."

God is all for second chances and being tolerant of each other's faults—considering He never cancels on us despite our many faults. That should be our example. Proverbs 17:9 says that if love is our motivation, we can cover over the offense of our friends. In other words, if we remember and focus on *why* we host, gather, or spend time with friends, that reason will cover

over any disappointments or cancellations that may come our way. But if we dwell on the offense, it will turn to bitterness in our hearts and frustration in our heads—and perhaps even create a wall between friends.

So when friends cancel last minute, invite God into that disappointment and ask Him to remind you of your initial purpose for gathering with friends. What is your why? Is it a desire for connection? A longing for fun or entertainment? Love for the people around you? Whatever it is, hold on to that! And be present and caring to the friends who do show up. Then, when another opportunity arises to host or extend an invitation, you can do so with confidence, knowing that the reason you gather is a firm foundation, even if the guest list is not always within your control.

Friendspiration

WHEN INSECURITY STRIKES

Whenever I sense a shift in a friendship and feel like I am not a priority to that person, I try to speak this over myself: God created me for true friendship, I am worthy of true friendship, and I am a good friend.

Reflect

Think of a time when you counted on a friend to show up only for that person to cancel on you. How did it make you feel? How can that experience inspire you to change how you approach your friend commitments in the future?

Prayer

Lord, it hurts when a friend bails on me at the last minute. The next time it happens, help me see their side of the story. Help me have empathy and grace for friends when their busy schedules interrupt good plans. If the last-minute canceling becomes a habit, give me the courage to speak honestly with my friends about how it makes me feel when they don't show up. And, Lord, allow me to be considerate in my own yeses so that I don't overpromise to my friends. I want there to be mutual respect between me and my friends when it comes to showing up for each other. Amen.

Knowing Your True Worth

**I praise you because I am fearfully
and wonderfully made;
your works are wonderful,
I know that full well.**
—PSALM 139:14

As a Bible study leader, I take pride in creating thoughtful experiences to help people connect. I had thought the attendees always appreciated my efforts until I received some hurtful feedback. One girl let me know there were a few members talking behind my back who weren't happy with how the study was going.

This information seemed to come out of nowhere, and it certainly sent me into a deep spiral: *I am a terrible person, and all the women think so too.* Rather than adjusting some agenda items in the schedule, I began to question my value as a person. Their perception of me became more important than who God says I am. Doubt creeped in on my spiritual giftings, made me feel like I didn't measure up, and sent me into the overdrive of wanting to please everyone.

A few weeks later, I attended a retreat with the personal goal of processing disappointments from the year. In a room full of women I didn't know, I had no reason to be anything other than my imperfect self. I could sit and sip my tea without worrying about impressing the people around me. During my time alone, God revealed to me how I was allowing my friends' criticism to define my value.

As women, we often find ourselves trying to please our peers by shaping our behaviors and personalities to be more likable. So when a friend offers her unsolicited—or solicited—thoughts and opinions about who we are or what we do, that feedback can reveal how little control we actually have over the edited versions we think we're presenting to the world. (Wait, my friends don't think I'm perfect?)

While friends can bring great value to your life, they do not define your value. What a slippery slope it is to put your friends on a seat of judgment to decide how important, beautiful, needed, or funny you are or are not. Thankfully, God does not require you to prove your value to Him—He already declares you wonderful and worthy. And when you base your worth and identity in how God sees you, you won't ever need to prove your value to your peers. You can be who you are—weaknesses and all—and trust that your friends' feedback won't make or break how you feel about yourself . . . or how you think your friends feel about you overall. Especially when you feel like God has you exactly where He wants you.

After my restorative retreat, I decided to find more centering moments that connected me to my God-given identity, like taking walks and praying or listening to worship music while making dinner. For you, a centering activity could involve painting, crocheting, working a puzzle, exercising, writing, or baking. Whatever allows you to sit in the fullness of God's love for you, make sure you set aside time for it. These hobbies or activities—while not end goals in themselves—can help bring us a sense of calm and remind us that we are loved and we are enough just as we are.

In the case of my Bible study, I eventually realized that, while my friends may have wanted our study to look different, they weren't asking me to be a different person. Unfortunately, before I came to this conclusion, I made the mistake of taking the criticism and transferring it from the Bible study agenda to myself. I believed *I* was the problem—not the way the study was structured. That perspective could have been extremely damaging if I had kept believing it, and the same is true for any criticism that has been directed at you.

Rather than obsessing about how worthy or unworthy other people might find you, choose to be content in knowing God doesn't require perfection. Since He knows everything about you, He has no expectations of you and therefore can't ever be disappointed in what you do or don't do. So while we shouldn't be closed off to all negative feedback, we should be wary of allowing others' opinions to pull us off course. Instead, remember that our value comes from living in the love God has for us.

Friendspiration

CANCELING PLANS THOUGHTFULLY

Extending an invitation is a vulnerable step. You never know if people are going to come, *nor* do you know how hard it will be to follow through when you feel like you might not be bringing your best self. God sees your frustrations and fears in both roles.

So when you're the one feeling paralyzed over whether you should cancel or not, cast yourself in your friend's shoes and let your "yes" be yes and your "no" be no. Life gets busy, and plenty of legitimate things do come up unexpectedly in our schedules. So when you do need to cancel:

Rather than just not showing up, let your friend know that something came up last minute and that you will not be able to attend. Apologize and tell your friend how much they mean to you and how much you wanted to be able to keep your plans. Explain how you appreciate all the time they put into planning and hosting and express your desire to be able to come next time.

Make it right. Find a time you can get together. Be specific and set a date so it isn't a passive invitation or a nice sentiment but a real desire to connect.

Reflect

When others criticize you or tell you who to be, how can you remind yourself of who God says you are? What truths from God can you call to mind?

Prayer

Lord, I confess all the ways I placed my friend's opinion of me above Your opinion of me. Help me to feel Your love for me so that I can shake off those hurtful criticisms and forgive myself and my friends when I let them rule my mind and heart. Your love for me is enough. Your love for me gives me worth that can never be taken away. Thank You, God. Amen.

WHEN A FRIEND *Is Always Busy*

Love is patient, love is kind.

—1 CORINTHIANS 13:4

My neighbors are my go-to friends for last-minute fun—proximity is very powerful! The husband and the kids are content and settled? Let's go tear up the neighborhood with leggings, the pace of a champion speed-walker, and a Stanley cup that has the size and enamel coating to fend off dehydration and anyone who dares to walk slowly in front of us.

Inspired by our previous hangouts together and hopeful for some uninterrupted chatting time, I texted a particular neighbor whom I hadn't connected with in a while. After I waited several hours, the response finally came through:

That doesn't fit into my schedule, sorry.

I put my phone down and began to wonder if this was just a really busy season for my friend, or if there was something else lurking behind the vague message. Either way, her answer to my invitation stung.

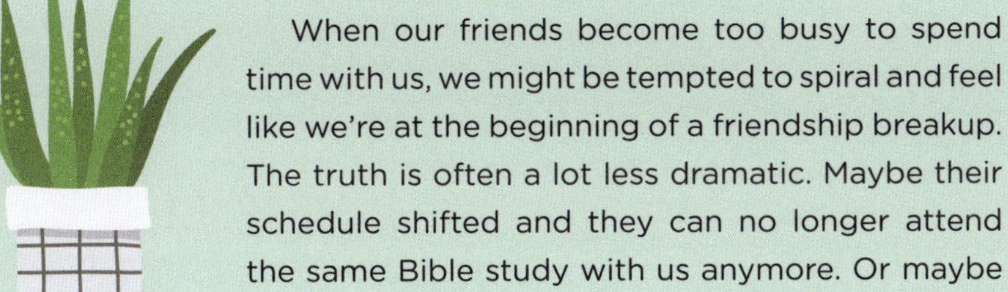

When our friends become too busy to spend time with us, we might be tempted to spiral and feel like we're at the beginning of a friendship breakup. The truth is often a lot less dramatic. Maybe their schedule shifted and they can no longer attend the same Bible study with us anymore. Or maybe they started a new job and can no longer do Saturday morning workouts. If they've recently gotten married or had a baby, perhaps they're restructuring their priorities so they can cultivate rhythms as a family. And as good as these new routines might be, they might also create tension in your friendship. As happy as you are for your friend, you can still find yourself mourning the schedule changes.

If you have experienced a friendship shift like this, you might be tempted to pull away. To push that friendship to the back burner and focus on an easier friendship. But when you truly love and care about a friend, you'll want to come up with a creative solution that suits your respective schedules.

Loving a friend through life's transitions can be done in a lot of ways, but Scripture reminds us that love is patient and kind (see 1 Corinthians 13:4). Instead of moving toward our knee-jerk reaction of pulling back, we can ask God: "How can I be patient and kind in understanding my friend and not place blame on her for canceling on me?" Instead of prejudging her, consider checking in on her. She could have a very valid reason for being suddenly busy or unavailable, and your showing grace to her could go a long way. If you begin with a favorable view instead of jumping to conclusions, you'll have a better chance of redirecting the friendship toward a healthy new rhythm for both of you.

When a friend's lack of attention to the friendship becomes more frequent even without a good reason, then it may be time to ask God if you should walk away from this friendship. Whatever the outcome of the friendship, you can find peace in knowing you have loved your friend and given her an opportunity to respond. You have done your part!

Reflect

When have you experienced grace from a friend during one of your own busy seasons? How can you approach your busy friends with patience and kindness?

Prayer

Lord, I'm having hurt feelings from a friend's busy season. Be a comfort to me so that I don't place all the blame on my friend. We all go through seasons where something drastically changes how we show up. Help me have grace for them, just like I'd want them to show grace toward me. Amen.

FRIENDIVERSARY

MATERIALS: n/a
PREP TIME: 3+ hours
DATE TIME: 1–3 days
FRIENDS NEEDED: 1+

Celebrating a friendiversary all started with my friend Melanie, the most intentional friend I know. We met over ten years ago, when we were tasked with chopping dozens of onions for a church elder retreat. The elder's wife passed us each a pair of ski goggles to keep our eyes from burning and said, "Good luck!" Thus, a friendship was born with ski goggles on our faces and onion smell on our hands. Which shows that making new friends doesn't always have to be glamorous.

We have since continued to mark the occasion of our friendship anniversary every year with a fun hangout. But for our ten-year friendiversary, we went on a weekend trip to L.A. together. It was perfect. We each picked an activity we wanted to do (Melanie: Visit the Academy Award Museum; Bailey: Have lunch near my alma mater) and wrote each other appreciation letters to share. There may have even been a picture slideshow involved that allowed us to look back on our friendship over the years. We left L.A. planning our next big friendiversary outing.

Later, I was interviewed for a magazine, and the journalist was shocked that my friend and I would plan something so elaborate just for us. It seems crazy to take time away from a spouse or kids or work. But I believe friendships are just as important as some of our other valuable relationships.

So, as you reflect on certain friends that feel more like sisters, pick the month (or the day if you remember) of when you first started your friendship and plan a special time to celebrate what makes your friendship so unique and worthwhile.

Feeling Left Behind

We wait in hope for the Lord;
he is our help and our shield.
In him our hearts rejoice,
for we trust in his holy name.
May your unfailing love be with us, Lord,
even as we put our hope in you.
—PSALM 33:20–22

Have you ever felt left behind as you watch other friends make big moves in their careers, dating relationships, or spiritual lives? Sometimes it doesn't matter where you are in your own journey; it can be difficult to be content as the friends around you are making plans and moving forward. When it feels like everyone else is leaving one stage of life for the next, you might assume they are leaving you behind. How will you ever catch up? *God, how long will You make me wait for my turn?*

Even in elementary school, I remember how awful it felt to be left behind when a group of girls would run off to the playground while I was still fumbling in the hallway trying to wrestle my jean jacket out of my locker. Now as an adult, I struggle with watching my friends enter new stages of life I had hoped to walk through with them, only to find myself still wrestling to figure out my next move. In these situations, I

want to feel joy for my friends while simultaneously wishing they'd slow down so I could catch up.

As the one who moved ahead faster than my friends in several areas, I had a different perspective of feeling left behind. Because I was married and had children in an earlier stage of life, I quickly recognized the chasm between my single friends and myself. They could often drop what they were doing to spend time together, while I needed to check in on and prioritize the growing relationships in my own home. I felt like my friends weren't willing to meet me in my season, and I was running out of steam trying to meet them in theirs.

Lasting friends learn to be flexible and patient as they watch friends move ahead while they are still waiting for God to answer prayers for them. The sentiment of slowing down to understand and give grace for the other person's life stage is like an elementary friend saying, "I'll wait for you while you get your jacket," or an adult friend saying, "We may be in completely different seasons, but I'm patient enough to learn about yours." God might be moving you and your friends at different paces in life, but instead of feeling resentful in your season, try to discover how you can be there for each other. And while you wait or long to be where another friend might be, take this worry to God. Lean on Him while you ask the questions, *"Why isn't it my turn to have a baby, to be invited on a friend trip, to be trusted to lead the Bible study, to move into a new house with my husband, or to have someone I can call my best friend?"*

God is your help and shield while you wait, so instead of grumbling, sow joy in your season and rejoice with your friends in *their* seasons. God can graciously grant you the contentment to feel like you are exactly where you are meant to be. And we can all work together to see how our differing seasons can support each other.

Now, as my kids are older and all my friends are having babies, I have a lot more capacity to make dinner for those new parents and be present for them. I wouldn't have had that if we had all been sleepless and overwhelmed together. This lesson has taught me to see differing seasons as a challenge in empathy. Instead of feeling left behind, we can choose to see how our unique journeys stretch us to help our friends through new seasons.

Reflect

Where do you feel left behind? Has it caused any bitterness toward your friends? How can you trust God to sow joy in your and your friends' unique seasons?

Prayer

Lord, help me to sow seeds of contentment while I wait on You to open the door for my next thing. Help me to have genuine joy for my friends who are experiencing new big things and to not jump to feeling left behind just because You are moving them at a different pace. Help me develop more trust in Your timing as You move things into place for me. Amen.

Friend Date

PRAYER BANNER

MATERIALS: paper and pens
PREP TIME: 5 minutes
DATE TIME: 1 hour
FRIENDS NEEDED: 1+

The first time I heard of a prayer banner was at a friend's baby shower. Each friend took a pennant and wrote down a prayer for labor that we could string up in the delivery room. This was an intentional act of love from one friend to another, and though it was for a specific occasion, it can also be a meaningful girls' night activity at any stage of life and for any occasion.

The details of this friend date include purchasing some paper for pennants, colored pens, and ribbon. Then ask your friends to bring some of their favorite supplies to add *zhuzh* to the pennants—glitter glue, printed pictures, paint, etc. Create one banner for each girl by having your guests write one pennant prayer for each attendee. The prayer pennants may include a scripture, a word, or a one-sentence prayer. Spend some time at the beginning of your friend date to allow each guest to share a specific prayer request they have in their season. This creates a more personal prayer banner.

This friend date reminds me of this verse: "Let his banner over me be love" (Song of Songs 2:4), because the craft is a tangible reminder to your friends that they are covered in love through prayer and God's Word. When your friends look up in their dorm rooms, office cubicles, or even bathrooms, they can remember how you are there cheering them on in prayer.

The Weight of Your Words

Do not let any unwholesome talk come out of your mouths, but only what is helpful for building others up according to their needs, that it may benefit those who listen.

—EPHESIANS 4:29

We all know how badly it hurts when people we trust say things that cut us deeply. Yet how often do we talk poorly about or to our friends? Perhaps it stems from jealousy ("Did you see how Kelly was flaunting her new kitchen in those pictures?"), a desire to have others join us in a bad mood ("That movie was so dumb; I don't know why you like it so much."), or a twisted satisfaction in knocking down someone else's choices to affirm our own decisions ("She's delusional to think that her kids need all the new tech gear."). However it reveals itself, we all have a dark side. In many ways, we're just one text away from being as bad as our favorite TV villains.

A few comments tossed around in jest may seem innocent but can stick with us for a lifetime. I can remember what girls said about me from playground days nearly thirty years ago all because I fell victim to someone else's careless words. No doubt you have your own stories of how a mean comment left a lasting impact. Because we likely have our own hurts from the harmful or petty words thrown our way, we should be extra aware of how we use our words.

Scripture tells us that our tongue is our greatest weapon: "With the tongue we praise our Lord and Father, and with it we curse human beings, who have been made in God's likeness" (James 3:9). As women, I think we understand this one well. When a woman wants to wage warfare on another, all she needs to do is open her mouth and begin to spread rumors. Sometimes even what is "meant" to be interpreted as a joke still ends up tearing someone else down.

Even in Christian circles and among our closest friends, we can behave this way. "Out of the same mouth come praise and cursing. My brothers and sisters, this should not be" (James 3:10). These cutting remarks, often dished out carelessly, can leave an awful, achy feeling afterward—both for the recipient *and* the speaker. So how can we protect ourselves and our friends from quick or thoughtless words?

One way to guard against negativity is to consider and choose words that will build one another up. If you know you're heading into a conversation with a friend who tends to push your buttons, choose some positive or encouraging things to focus on before your time together. If you notice your jealousy flaring up, ask for God's grace and try to redirect your envy into gratitude for your friend's success. If you're just having a bad day, take a moment to calm your breath and list some of the blessings you can be thankful for.

Of course, even with the best planning, you can't always control what will come out of your mouth in a heated moment. What you *can* control is asking God to help you pay attention to your words and the effect they have on others, so the next time you feel the mean girl urge, you'll be less likely to act on it. You can also ask yourself if you would say the thing you want to say in front of your children, your nieces or nephews, a mentor, or anyone else you respect. These are great checks! But most importantly, would you say this in front of God? Especially about someone He has made in His image? God sees and cares for each person just as He cares for you, so we shouldn't speak poorly of anyone. Even when we mess up, God does not define us by our faults or use them to cut us down. Rather, He uses His words to breathe life into us. May we do the same!

Friendspiration

WHEN YOU NEED TO APOLOGIZE

We all mess up and get caught saying hurtful things, and when we do, apologizing helps. As soon as you recognize your mistake, apologize. Don't let the harmful words linger too long. Instead, address them right away.

You might say, "I shouldn't have spoken that way to you. It was not my place. It came from my own insecurity. I am sorry." Or you could say, "Hey, I apologize for coming with a critical spirit today. I should not be talking about our friends this way. It's not kind or respectful. Could we change the topic?"

Humbly admitting where you crossed the line may not erase what you've said, but it will go a long way in bringing restoration from any hurt feelings between friends.

Reflect

How can we use God's example and speak life over our friends? What are some practical ways to help keep yourself from speaking poorly about your friends?

Prayer

Lord, I confess all the ways I have used my words to cut others down. I know it comes from a sinful heart and my motivations are not pure. When the temptation comes to respond unkindly, help me to keep my mouth shut and to consider the effect of my words. Guide me in remembering Your love and care for me, so I can better love my friends from a place of wholeness. Amen.

WHEN YOU WANT TO *Outshine Your Friends*

As God's chosen people, holy and dearly loved, clothe yourselves with compassion, kindness, humility, gentleness and patience. . . . And over all these virtues put on love, which binds them all together in perfect unity.

—COLOSSIANS 3:12, 14

My publishing journey took many years to work out. My first literary agent retired. My second agent quit. By my third agent, I wondered if I would ever accomplish my writing goals. To make matters even more discouraging, several of my friends who had started the writing journey with me were getting not just one book deal but multiple deals. Why them and not me? Were they funnier than me? More talented? Were they really that much better at writing than I was?

Needless to say, I was jealous.

Jealousy may be one of the biggest threats to a solid friendship, because nothing will kill a friendship faster than thinking your friend has *more* than you—more wealth, family, health, beauty, accomplishments, friends (the list goes on)—especially if you're already feeling insecure about how little you think you have in any of those areas. That insecurity, combined with jealousy and fed by the enemy's whispered lie that "you need to prove you're just as good or better," can often push you into believing you have to outshine your friends in order to be accepted.

The enemy likes for us to believe our friends are the true enemy. As a result, we compare and divide and treat one another with contempt. Or even worse, we doubt our own God-given value or the truth that we are loved by Him just as we are. Unfortunately, once we've forgotten how loved we are, we can find it difficult to love others because we are so busy trying to prove just how lovable we can be.

As believers, we should feel an urgency to fight against the enemy's tricks that create divisions between us and our friends. His lies might seem obvious at a distance, but in the moment, when tensions are high, we might struggle to discern fact from feeling. Are those two friends closer to each other than they are to you? Is that friend's success starting to make her self-centered? Does that friend think she's "beyond" you now, because she's achieved the dream you've both talked about for so long?

Colossians 3 urges us to put on compassion, kindness, humility, gentleness, and patience—*not* jealousy or envy. Our reactions and attitudes can convey a range of mindsets to those around us depending on how we clothe ourselves. When we wrap ourselves in God's love (like wearing a superhero costume), we can become agents of love that fight jealousy and hate. Even when the enemy comes against us with tricks and disguises, we are able to withstand being fooled and can instead seek unity over division.

One of my writing friends, Kelsey, is the epitome of someone who supports other women in their entrepreneurial endeavors. She is so secure in who she is that her ability to lift other women up beside her is inspiring. She took me—a wannabe writer at the time—and made me into a credible voice others wanted to listen to, because she generously shared her business tricks and tips. She could have easily hoarded that knowledge for herself, but she chose kindness instead.

When she told me about landing her first book deal (before I had mine), she leaned over on the couch and said, "You are going to get this. You are an amazing communicator. We will be celebrating you next." And she was right. She believed in me and showed me that generosity is more enriching to a friendship than jealousy.

So when you're tempted to reach for jealousy when one of your friends gets a win, remember that God loves you . . . and her, and her, and her. You are on the same team, invited to celebrate your wins and her wins (because they're really all God's wins anyway). Let's ask God to give us wisdom to see our jealousy and squash it with love.

Besides, comparison is so last year.

Reflect

Where do you see jealousy coming between you and your friends? How can you clothe yourself in the type of virtues Colossians 3:12–14 mentions?

Prayer

Lord, here I am again, caught in the tangle of jealous emotions. I love these friends of mine, and yet I still find myself looking for reasons to put them down to make myself feel better. Instead, help me to find my acceptance and worth in You, Lord. That way, I don't need to boast about how great I am but can, in humility, lift the friends around me. Amen.

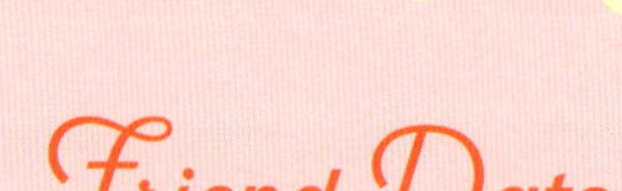

Friend Date

LUMINARY LOOK-BACKS

MATERIALS: white paper bags, battery-powered candles, markers

PREP TIME: 5–10 minutes

DATE TIME: 1–2 hours

FRIENDS NEEDED: 4+

Every year, take time to reflect and look back on all that God has done for you and through you. I believe this helps us remember God's goodness, despite the many days that feel tough.

A luminary look-back is a DIY craft involving a white paper bag and some markers. As you gather with friends, take some time to draw, write, and color your bag with different moments you want to recognize and remember from the last year or season. Once everyone is finished decorating, turn on the candles and put them inside the bags to glow. Friends can take their luminary home and light it up for several nights, as they remember where they were and how they've grown. May these luminary look-backs be an example that, even in the darkness, God's light shines through.

WHEN FRIENDSHIP ENDS *for a Reason*

**He will cover you with his feathers,
and under his wings you will find refuge;
his faithfulness will be your shield and rampart.**
—PSALM 91:4

"Where do you see our friendship going from here?" I asked.

"I think we have had too many years to just give up on it altogether, but I can't treat you the way I treat my other friends based off of our past conflict," she said.

My heart sank, and I had to fight to get the next words out: "Then I don't think I see us being friends at all."

Then one of my closest friends got into her car and drove away.

I wasn't sure why this friendship had taken such a sharp turn, but as I reflected on it, I saw all the moments that had led to this conversation.

I had been grasping to keep the friendship alive because it just seemed to make sense: We shared the same faith, we shared similar interests, and we had spent so many great moments together. Of course, we'd had some bad moments, too, but I had explained those icky memories away as best as I could. After all, both of us had invested a lot of time and energy into the friendship, and I wanted to hold on to it.

But when our continued conflict and her unhealthy patterns finally reached a tipping point, I knew God had led me to say goodbye. Since I hadn't had the courage to make the decision throughout all our years of conflict, I could feel that God was the one guiding my steps.

Sometimes we end up in friendships that cycle through the ups and downs. Seeing the long-term effects of this relationship seesaw can be difficult when we're in the middle of it. Often, it's not until God removes that person from our life that we can see why He did so. Other times, we may never understand why the friendship had to end.

A girlfriend once told me, "Rejection is God's protection." She felt that whenever she received any kind of rejection in her life, God was the one protecting her and saving her for something better and more spiritually healthy. Based on my experience in friendships, I think she's onto something.

When it feels like a friend has backed off from a friendship, God might be removing this friend for a particular reason we can't identify. But in the pain and confusion of not knowing all the details, we can still hold to the truth that God is with us. He can take hurtful experiences and transform them into space to welcome friendships that may be a better fit.

If you have recently (or ever) walked through a friendship breakup, let me just say I'm so sorry. Losses like these were never part of God's plan for you . . . or anyone. Being a friend is hard, and being a friend in relationship with other complex people is even harder. But we have access to a God-given calm even in our friendship breakups, because He's tender to our wounds. As hard as breakups are, may you find some peace in knowing that Jesus loves you and loves her—He has not chosen sides. My prayer as you walk through this season is that you find refuge in God's arms and in the arms of caring friends. God will be faithful to comfort you.

Reflect

How have you had to trust God in friendships that have ended? If you're sensing that a friendship breakup might be on its way, how can you prayerfully approach it?

Prayer

Lord, You are good even when I can't see it. You are watching over me and showering Your love on me, even when I am walking through difficult things. Help me to let go of some of the pain from a recently ended friendship and trust that You will open more doors for me to experience new friends. Be a soothing balm to the rejection I feel, and help me find peace in Your protection. Amen.

From Frenemy to Friend

To you who are listening I say: Love your enemies, do good to those who hate you, bless those who curse you, pray for those who mistreat you. If someone slaps you on one cheek, turn to them the other also. If someone takes your coat, do not withhold your shirt from them. Give to everyone who asks you, and if anyone takes what belongs to you, do not demand it back. Do to others as you would have them do to you.

—LUKE 6:27–31

Sometimes the people we trust can wear the guise of a "frenemy"—a person in our social circle who seems to have it in for us. Can we love them even when there is so much tension between us?

One frenemy of mine sprouted up in my small group. I didn't know if it was my bubbly attitude that rubbed her the wrong way or if she felt like she didn't measure up to something she saw in me. Maybe she rolled her eyes at every person she knew, or she just didn't like me. Whatever the reason, our personalities and values didn't line up, and I felt an edge to our friendship. When I'd see her name on a guest list, my heart rate would speed up, and

I'd be hit with anxious thoughts about wanting to please her so she wouldn't dislike me so much.

Eventually, I had the opportunity to do a small intensive Bible study, and she was one of the people I asked to join (not a coincidence, since I really did want to know her and break down some of our hostile barriers). To my surprise, she said yes. Early on Tuesday mornings, four of us would get together to study God's Word, pray for one another, and share our hearts. The experience changed us and our friendship for the better, and although we didn't become best friends, we weren't frenemies anymore either.

What about you? Do frenemies exist in your circle? Are there people who take advantage of your kindness? Does anyone in your small group seem more like a foe than a friend? Are there friends of friends who make you feel unwanted in a friendship?

Wherever frenemies are involved, we feel like we *must* meet resistance with more resistance, whether a snarky comment with another snarky comment or gossip to win more people to our side. Yet God calls us out of our insecurities and preconceived notions and asks us to do the unthinkable—to love our frenemies. Jesus says, "Do good to those who hate you, bless those who curse you, pray for those who mistreat you" (Luke 6:27–28). What is He even talking about? He wants me to bless and pray for the people who are making my social life extra hard? Turns out, that's exactly what He wants us to do.

Praying for our frenemies helps give us eyes to see the person as God sees them—loved and valuable. Starting with the act of prayer reminds us to focus on God's love and forgiveness. And when we meditate on this truth (whether we fully *feel* that love or not), the action itself will begin to take root.

We'll find ourselves wanting to know the heart of this person and the characteristics that make them who they are. Curiosity and openness are the first steps. The more we know someone, the harder it is to dislike them or totally write them off. Of course, it takes willingness and time to understand one another. But being willing to show kindness when someone else shows pettiness is another opportunity to show God's mercy.

Loving your frenemy may make you uneasy, but this act allows you to participate in a small way in the unconditional love of Jesus, who somehow was able to love even the people who betrayed, tortured, and killed Him. He is always kind and gracious, even to the ungrateful (see Luke 6:35). Thankfully so, because we ourselves are not guiltless! We hurt others. We have played the frenemy in someone else's narrative. We have also wronged God, but He still welcomes us back with open arms. May this truth grow our humility, our mercy, and our ability to love even when it's not deserved.

Jesus ends this portion of Scripture with the directive to "do to others as you would have them do to you." Imagine how you would like to be received on your worst day: with a smile, a warm reception, and an attempt at friendly conversation, right? So the next time you see your frenemy, ask God to help you share His mercy and love with that person. And who knows? Maybe your foe will turn into a friend!

Reflect

How does a frenemy's presence make you feel when you're in a social setting? What is one way you can seek to know that person better?

Prayer

Lord, thank You for the mercy You show us when we turn away from You. I am the original frenemy in our relationship, and You still called me into friendship. Help me to see frenemies less as enemies and more as opportunities to stretch my friend skills by being polite and genuinely kind toward them. When a frenemy feels extra hard, help me discern when to lean in and when to back away, trusting You will work through the tension I feel with them. Amen.

PRAYER FOR
a Broken Friendship

**He heals the brokenhearted
and binds up their wounds.**
—PSALM 147:3

Lord,

I feel breathless, as though the pain in my chest from acknowledging the end of this friendship has knocked the wind out of me. It feels like I am running away from every bad word spoken and every awful way I felt in our last conversation.

I can't seem to find a moment to stop and rest from the negative memories that keep popping up in my mind. I can't stop overthinking every moment from the last few months or wondering if I was the one who made all the mistakes. Were the things she whispered about me behind my back and the critical words she said about me to my face true? Does everyone else think I am a bad friend too? Is her rejection valid?

I thought this person and I would be forever friends, but now I'm not sure we can be. Or even if I want us to be. I thought she would be present at all my important milestones, just like she has been before, but now it feels inauthentic to put on a smile just to pretend like nothing is fragmented between us.

You know what we've been through together and the ways we've brought positive change to each other's lives. But you also know the ways we've hurt each other and the ways we've been hurt by each other. I know you can fix anything, but I'm not sure how this can be fixed.

Come heal the wounds left by this broken friendship. I know you see me and can take irreparable situations and mend them—providing comfort for my hurting heart even though I still have questions and doubts. I so desperately need respite from the questions and doubts. Come heal the insecurities I feel in social situations where she might turn up. Help me navigate this new reality with grace and kindness even if I carry the hurt inside.

I confess the hurt I contributed to the friendship. Give me the courage to apologize if necessary. I confess the moments I've ranted and gossiped about her to my other friends, because I secretly hoped they'd side with me over her. In all honesty, I just wanted her to feel as low as I feel. I know she is Your daughter, God. You love her. I need to respect her as a sister in Christ, but I can't do that from a place of woundedness. Please grant me Your tenderness in respecting her and the way I speak about her to others.

Lord, help me to release the friendship and the "what ifs" and the "what could have been." Help me to forgive the hurt done toward me and give me the courage to show true forgiveness. Help me one day see the friendship through a lens of appreciation and not pain.

Amen.

Blooming

I pray that you, being rooted and established in love, may have power, together with all the Lord's holy people, to grasp how wide and long and high and deep is the love of Christ, and to know this love that surpasses knowledge—that you may be filled to the measure of all the fullness of God.

—EPHESIANS 3:17–19

Devoted to One Another in Love

Be devoted to one another in love. Honor one another above yourselves.

—ROMANS 12:10

Take a deep breath—you've arrived at a season where your friendship calendar feels full and where you've created regular rhythms for connection. New friends are turning into real friends. The memories are turning into inside jokes, and the sparse text thread has turned into an ongoing conversation. You have a committed group of friends—which is not easy to do in adulthood—so let the celebrations begin!

What makes this season extra special is when you have a group of friends who devote themselves to knowing God and one another more intimately and who faithfully invest in community while the rest of the world is investing in their careers, hobbies, or other self-interests. This type of tight-knit community has shown up in my life with friendships forged through going to church on Sundays, hosting fun game nights, and sharing a regular meal together. We chat about prayer requests over FaceTime and meet early in the morning for Bible study. We share our baby gear when one child grows out of it and pass it around the group. Seasons like this, where I find myself in the company of like-minded friends who are committed to one another, make my heart feel full.

When everything in your friendships is going perfectly, the temptation is often to slide into passivity and even laziness. If we're content in our friendships, we shouldn't need to put much work or effort into them, right? Well, no. If you had a garden and all your plants were blooming beautifully, that wouldn't convince you to stop watering or weeding them, would it?

Healthy and growing friendships are definitely blessings to celebrate, but they also offer us unique opportunities to lean closer and go deeper. Devoting yourself to one another can include agreeing to look past an offense because you can afford to love the friend even when you don't agree on everything. It can look like making friends feel like family by coming up with unique traditions out of a desire to mutually care for one another. It can look like planning a fun event to celebrate a new milestone in your friend's life, even when you're still waiting for your turn to reach that milestone.

The word *devote* means to give all or a large portion of your resources in dedication to something or someone else. And in this case, that resource is *love.* To love our friends from the depths of the love we experience from God is a gift. It is an honor to love our friends without expecting anything in return, simply because we are secure enough to go all in and give our friends our best.

So in this celebratory season, may your friends honor your efforts. May you carve out time and share your resources to invest in each other. And may you trust the bond of friendship to hold tight, because you are all in it together! The gift of blooming friendships is learning that giving love is the true foundation of joy. Not the trendy hangout spot. Not the cool pictures you took for social media. Not the things this friend can give you. It's the shared love between you.

Reflect

Which friend or friends have brought joy to you in this season? Send them a text of what you love about them or what you're grateful for in your friendship with them.

Prayer

Lord, thank You for this season that I've prayed and waited for. I feel so much joy and gratitude and peace for the friends who give me so much support and love. Help me to continue to love and honor the people You have entrusted to me in this season. I'm excited for this time of my life and what You'll do through these friendships. Amen.

Friend Date

THANK-YOU DINNER

MATERIALS: thank-you notes, meal of your choice, additional little gift (optional)
PREP TIME: 45–60 minutes
DATE TIME: 2 hours
FRIENDS NEEDED: 2+

My phone beeped with a text from one of my friends, and I saw she was inviting me to a mysterious lunch at her house. There were no details other than to show up on time. Intrigued, I arrived at her home to find eight women seated around a table that was beautifully decorated. My friend then explained how she wanted to throw us a thank-you lunch for being such great friends. She made a charming lunch and spoiled us with unique gifts. She then wrote each of us an encouraging letter about what she appreciated in our friendship and read them out loud to the table. I was stunned by the whole experience and vowed I would do this one day for my friends.

Surprising and spoiling your friends is an instant feel good. You could put out fancy candleholders and nice champagne flutes you haven't used in a year. Or meet at the local coffee shop with some flowers and a card. Write down some words on a notecard or give a formal speech. However you spin it, the surprise element is probably my favorite piece to this friend date.

Doing Life Together

Whether I come and see you or only hear about you in my absence, I will know that you stand firm in the one Spirit, striving together as one for the faith of the gospel without being frightened in any way by those who oppose you.

—PHILIPPIANS 1:27–28

If the world had its way, we would treat everything as a race or a competition: Who can get that promotion first? Who will get engaged first? Who will have the best wedding? Who will own a home first? Can you imagine how awful it would be if someone actually handed out medals for those sorts of things? Having real friendships would be nearly impossible, since we'd all be too busy constantly comparing ourselves to each other's achievements.

But isn't that often what we do?

Instead of partnering together, we look for small ways to diminish what God is doing in our friends' lives because we're unsure of what God is doing in us. For example, when a friend finds a career they are excited to pursue, we may brush it off as "a passing phase," since we're still stuck in that "finding yourself" season. Or we might downplay the opportunity a friend is given by being asked to lead another Bible study, because we've never been asked once. Or if a single friend tells us she met someone she hopes to spend more time with, we might feel spiteful enough to change the subject every time she brings up her new love interest. This should not be the way we live. The world is hard enough on us as women that we don't need to be hard on each other.

A friend of mine always makes me feel seen in my ministry roles as a wife, mother, neighbor, co-worker, and friend. Her support gives me the confidence to have heartfelt conversations with those who do not know Jesus. Her words of wisdom help me sort out an emotional motherhood moment. Her reminders to pray about political issues or to sort out a frustration I have with a co-worker without compromising my faith values are exactly what I need to continue living out the gospel each day. I wouldn't want to do life without her. We are like a little ministry team of two as we strive together for the faith of the gospel.

When we are walking with the Spirit, we can see there is no competition when it comes to living as women of God. We are all running our unique races toward Jesus and for God's glory. That common goal should unite us rather than divide us. So, no matter what you are doing—in the workplace, the home, the neighborhood—try to authentically support the friends around you. You may be carrying a lot of responsibilities or feel weighed down by expectations from yourself and others. But when you know you have a support system around you, you are more likely to keep striving after the passions and people God has entrusted to you. The best things you can do are things done in partnership with others.

The enemy should be afraid of us and what we can accomplish together. So link arms in unified sisterhood against the competitiveness the world would have us feel toward each other. The best part of "striving together as one for the faith of the gospel" is coming to the finish line together—not having held people back to get ahead, but allowing God to do a good work in all of us in a true spirit of friendship.

Reflect

Who has God entrusted to you to support and root for? How might you cultivate a spirit of championing others instead of falling into competitiveness with them?

Prayer

Lord, thank You for my friends who are ministry partners to me. Thank You for the friends who cheer me on with genuine joy for me. Help me to continue to support the women around me instead of letting jealousy take over our teamwork. Amen.

USING YOUR GIFTS *to Serve Others*

Each of you should use whatever gift you have received to serve others, as faithful stewards of God's grace in its various forms.

—1 PETER 4:10

In many ways, our friends and their unique gifts and talents can be compared to a box of crayons. All the crayons share the purpose of being coloring tools, but each one is a different shape and color. Similarly, each color is important, though some colors are called upon more frequently than others. Still, all are necessary to create a vibrant and complete picture of the Creator's love and unique design in the world.

When you think of your friendships, what unique giftings do you see in them? For me, I have friends who are skilled in administration, thoughtful in hospitality, wise in discernment, and creative in loving their neighbors. Each of them adds so much to my life and provides a fuller picture of God's grace in using every person to build His kingdom.

Some of us may know exactly where we fit when it comes to using our gifts. Others of us may still be navigating what our spiritual gifts might be and how we can contribute to our community. One way to discover your unique gifting is to think about what brings you joy and

how you can use that to serve others. If you're a master chef or baker, consider how you might share your cooking and baking skills for community events or with friends who might need a meal or a pick-me-up. If you're super organized, offer to plan the next friend retreat or book club. If you love performing acts of service, try popping by a friend's house to help with spring cleaning or volunteering to give pedicures at the next group hangout. No matter what you've identified as your "God thing," be a faithful steward of God's grace in your gifts and offer them freely.

God has blessed your community with talents and particular characteristics that are uniquely designed to serve your specific group of friends, in this specific season, for these specific needs. As you reflect on the collection of gifts represented in your social circle, you will begin to see how God has arranged each person to serve the needs of others. He situates each of you for the good of the community.

Seeing how your friend group all fits together is like putting all the crayons back in the box and seeing that there is a spot for each one. Together, you are a complete set.

Reflect

How has God uniquely gifted you? How can you use your spiritual gifts in this season to serve the people around you?

Prayer

Lord—wow, You have blessed me with so many talented friends. I feel so full when I remember each of them and the ways they add to our community. Help me to not be complacent about using my gifts but to continue to find fresh ways to serve my friends in my unique way. Help me remember that my part is important to the whole. Amen.

Friendspiration

RECOGNIZING EACH OTHER'S GIFTS

How easily are you able to identify your friends' gifts? If this is something you struggle with, try asking yourself where you see your friends' passions meeting the needs of the community or noticing when they come most alive. What looks easy to them but is hard for others?

You could also take a night to gather and encourage your friends by identifying and praying over each other's gifts.

Openness to Change

I am convinced that neither death nor life, neither angels nor demons, neither the present nor the future, nor any powers, neither height nor depth, nor anything else in all creation, will be able to separate us from the love of God that is in Christ Jesus our Lord.

—ROMANS 8:38–39

When I first became a mother, I pushed against the notion that having a baby would change my friendships. Although people say *everything* changes when you have a child, I figured I could at least control how I showed up in my friendships. Unfortunately (as you might have guessed), this effort to stay as connected as I had been before kids left me feeling very exhausted, unseen, and defeated. Nobody seemed to understand what I was walking through, nor did they see my struggle to keep up with the façade that nothing would ever change our friendships. As I soon learned, my plan lacked faith that my friends would be loyal to me no matter what season of life I was walking through.

Shifts in our personal lives can often be perceived as threats to our friendships. Naturally, we don't want a disruption to alter the status quo, even if it's a good thing like a new relationship, a new job, a new school, or a new friend. But change is a natural part of life, and we need to be ready for it. We may not be able to stop the change, but we can decide ahead of time how we will react to the change. The *reaction* to the change will often prove whether the friendship will survive the shift or not.

When you're afraid of change, you will do everything possible to fight against it. Sometimes this avoidance leads to alienating yourself from the new milestone in your friend's life or pretending her new relationship doesn't exist, or even disparaging the new health journey she is on. As a result, you might miss an opportunity to meet that friend where she is in her new season. The alternative is to respond with curiosity and to look for new ways to connect with your friends despite the changes. If you're the one going through a change, you want friends who can withstand any unforeseen obstacles and remain willing to work through the shifts with you. This kind of sisterly love is not easily separated or broken.

Having walked through a variety of transitions myself and with my community, I know how to navigate changes a bit better. I no longer need to pretend that things haven't changed between me and my friends. Instead, I communicate how changes might affect our relationship so that there are no surprises or hurt feelings when the friendship feels different. I also recognize that the growing pains tend to be temporary. And when the transition "earthquakes" are over, my friends and I can discover new ways to connect.

When we have the creative freedom to approach our friendships in new ways, we are better equipped to prolong the life of our friendships. The world might encourage us to walk away from friendships that become too difficult to manage, but the family of God sticks together. We model a lifelong care for our friends because,

despite any changes, we will always have Jesus at the center. Everything else outside our control might change, but our shared faith will stand firm.

So bring on the transitions, because you're ready for them!

Reflect

How have you navigated changes in a healthy way and maybe a not-so-healthy way? What could you try as you move forward?

Prayer

Lord, You never change and Your love is lasting. This kind of love helps me understand what a lasting love for my friends looks like versus a fickle one. Remind me that I don't need to be afraid of the changes in our season of life, because if a friendship is really meant to last, it will. Help me to be creative in pursuing my friends and not allow momentary limitations to derail a history of friendship. Amen.

Friend Date

GAME NIGHT FOR GOOD

MATERIALS: games, food, and drinks
PREP TIME: 2 hours
DATE TIME: 2–3 hours
FRIENDS NEEDED: 5+

As much as we love a good time with friends, we should also consider the power our friendships have to give back. Hosting a charity game night is a great way to build connections with one another while doing something good for the community.

Try making this type of game night more formal by sending invitations and detailed instructions. Let your friends know exactly what you hope to achieve in your get-together by including the dollar amount required to play, the allotted time of the evening, and the incentive that the winning team at the end of the night will get to choose a charity to give the cash prize to. You may want to include some charities to consider on your invitation or allow your guests time to be thoughtful about which charity they would choose.

On the night of the event, select three to four team games that you can all play together throughout the evening (like Scattergories, Pictionary, etc.). Tally the points of each game won. Give the first-place winner five points, the second-place team three points, and the third-place team one point. You can also set this up as single-person teams, and the one winner will select the charity.

For extra fun, suggest to friends that they can dress like they are heading to a casino in Vegas. You can also cultivate a more relaxed environment by providing snacks or homemade cookies. The real win is doing good together.

Celebrate Always

Rejoice in the Lord always. I will say it again: Rejoice!
—PHILIPPIANS 4:4

When we were growing up, my group of friends found any reason to celebrate something. One summer, we celebrated a new trampoline in our friend's backyard by hosting a twenty-four-hour jump-a-thon. Some designed T-shirts and others created playlists. Some organized everyone's jump time slot and others planned snacks. At 6 P.M. on a Friday, we began jumping. Two sets of friends would take an hour slot. My hours were 11 P.M. and 1 A.M., and I bounced along to my favorite songs from the early 2000s with some of my favorite people. The next day, the jump-a-thon concluded with fifteen overtired friends.

I have a photo from that day, and it brings me so much joy because it reminds me of a time in my life when a group of people found every opportunity to celebrate life together—whether it was celebrating a favorite hangout spot like our beloved trampoline or cheering each other on at a sports event (even if we were on the B team). We never tired of finding something to celebrate (or making team shirts).

Though the trampoline story might sound silly, it offers a good reminder that we should create a culture that celebrates each other's wins—big or small. We should celebrate job promotions and pet birthdays. Answered prayers or completed presentations. New marriages or the perfect homemade sourdough recipe. The real beauty behind celebrating is twofold: You get to enjoy life *together* and you get to rejoice not in what you accomplished but in the joys God has given.

Sprinkling in celebrations makes the smallest victory feel like God's greatest win. So share good things with one another, have a party in your car with smoothies, drop off balloons at someone's door, or send a five-dollar gift card to someone to say, "You are doing a really great job—have a muffin on me." If I see a social media post from a friend announcing how they are proud of something they've done, I slip a note in the mail to let them know I saw and am impressed! While I was working on the edits of this book, a friend sent me flowers to tell me how proud she is of my hard work—I felt so seen!

In all things, remember that the Lord delights in you and in the little and big things you do. You can be an extension of that pure joy in the things happening in your friends' lives. So rejoice today! Celebrate the gifts God has given you! Recognize the blessing of having friends to celebrate those gifts with!

Reflect

What is one celebration you could plan for your friends this season?

Prayer

Lord, thank You for giving us little blessings in our lives just because You love us. Help me to have a spirit that celebrates others' wins and my own wins. No win should go unseen or uncelebrated. Grow in me a spirit of happiness for my friends when good things happen and build a culture of people who find ways to honor one another by celebrating Your good things, God. Amen.

The Spirit of Gratitude

Give thanks in all circumstances; for this is God's will for you in Christ Jesus.

—1 THESSALONIANS 5:18

When I see photos of other friend groups doing fun things together, I can become discontented. Those women have figured out how to balance girls' nights *and* parenting. Those friends have somehow orchestrated five schedules to all go on a camping trip together. Somehow they have time and energy to make the funniest videos together. It makes me wonder if I am as happy in my friendships as that friend group seems to be.

Seeing these types of things can cause me to feel like my friend group could be doing more. If I let myself go down this spiral, it paints the way I think about my friends with a hue of gray—a less colorful view of my friendships and the value of our relationship. It's only when I finally look up from my phone and notice the gift of my friends that I realize I'm so grateful for them. That gratitude quiets the noise.

At some point, friendships will experience a stall—when the growth in the friendship feels curbed. You might not connect as often, or you are unsure what the future of the friendship holds. When growth isn't happening in your friendship, you might be tempted to look at other friend circles and wonder why yours isn't more like the ones you see on social media. You might see special outings, social clubs, or friend trips and wonder why your friends don't do that together. Unfortunately, the desire to have your friendships look like others' will steal your joy and make you question the quality of your friendships.

Focusing on gratitude on a regular basis will help us fight against restlessness, discontentment, and comparison. This gratitude challenges us to pause and hand over to God the moments in our days when our expectations for friendship don't match up with our reality. Though there may not be anything dramatic or bad happening in our actual relationships, seeing a photo or comment from someone else may send us spiraling. Doing the inner work of practicing gratitude to heal our dissatisfaction will carry over into how we see ourselves in relation to our friends. Do we need them to text us all day to reassure us that our friendship is amazing? No! That's unreasonable. But our decision to pursue gratitude instead of wallowing in comparison allows us to push away the need to prove our friendships are in a good place.

How do you practice gratitude? If you need inspiration, try sitting with a journal open and writing down everything that comes to mind. Remember funny stories, the moments you cared for each other in hard times, and the things you love about your friends. Make a point of telling your friends specifically what they mean to you. The gratitude will come, especially when we take the time to remember.

You've got something good going for you—don't let anything come in and steal your joy!

Reflect

What are some specific things you're grateful for in your friendships right now?

Prayer

Lord, my friends are awesome, and we fit like a glove. We may be going through a season that feels a little stale, but every time we get together, I know it is making a lasting impact. Help breathe new life into my friendships. Rid me of the temptation to compare my friend group to things I see on social media. Those things aren't real. The friends you've given me are real. I am so grateful! Amen.

Friendspiration

NEW RHYTHMS

When things stall in your friendships, it may be time to shake things up. Change your rhythms and be open to finding new ways to connect.

I had to get creative with a friend of mine when we both went from being stay-at-home moms to working part-time. We could not align our schedules, so we started doing quarterly sleepovers with our entire families.

If your old rhythms for spending time together aren't working, try something new. Don't give up; instead, get creative!

Fighting for Togetherness

How good and pleasant it is
when God's people live together in unity!
—PSALM 133:1

"I have felt so confused about my faith lately, and I'm maybe a bit in a depressed state. I don't want to engage with the church right now," my friend shared with me.

It made me anxious to hear one of my longtime sisters in Christ sharing these raw feelings she felt toward God. I didn't know exactly what to say. But I remember telling her that I would be there for her as she explored her next step of faith.

A few days later, I called her to check in and left a message reminding her I was there for her in this struggle and would be praying against any spiritual attacks that were coming against her. She immediately responded with a text saying how I had hurt her by calling any of the things she was going through a spiritual attack. Without giving me a chance to apologize or hear her feelings and thoughts, she decided she wanted space from the friendship. As a result, a *decade*-old friendship ended over one misunderstanding. I was devastated.

In a season of blooming friendships, we should fight for harmony over discord. When we love people dearly, experiencing a harsh or insensitive word from them about the way we think or live is upsetting. We might disagree about how we raise our kids, how we engage in local politics, or what sports teams we support. We can also disagree about faith: the "right way" to worship, observe Sabbath, or tithe. All of these are important things, but none are more important than the friendship itself. When you disagree with your friends, you should aim to listen rather than shut each other down. This doesn't mean we should pretend that what they said didn't offend us or that we should say we're fine when we are far from it. Nor should we respond to our friend's next few invitations with short, ambivalent replies. These tactics are not healthy or helpful.

Instead, we should address the conflict immediately and ask our friend what the goal of the conversation might be. Maybe something like: "I hope we walk away having understood each other's position." Or "I just want to be heard right now." Reach for words that draw you closer together rather than create more distance.

James's wise words about being quick to listen and slow to speak are a great prayer to whisper to yourself when things get heated between you and your friends (see James 1:19). Honor your friends by putting aside your quick judgments and choosing your words thoughtfully. Respect the response your friend has chosen in the conflict. Maybe she needs time to think. But plan for a time to come back together for a follow-up so no one ghosts the other, which might result in a slow death to the friendship that is more painful than a tough conversation might be.

It is possible for us to disagree *and* stand on the foundation of our faith—Christ, in whom love, mercy, and forgiveness meet. This doesn't mean we thoughtlessly give up our opinions or values to create a fake harmony. We don't have to compromise our values to accommodate space for a friend to process their concerns. Seeking unity means looking beyond the issue and recognizing that there's more to our friend than the team they root for, the political affiliation they have, or the school they decided to send their kids to. There is a grace in allowing space for friends to apologize even if we don't come to a mutual agreement. True friends are worth a conversation to find common ground.

Aim to champion your friends and remain grounded in the knowledge that you still love each other, despite where you land. Strive for reconciliation over being right. The enemy does not want God's people to be unified, because when God's people are living in harmony, God speaks His blessings (see Psalm 133:3). So be on guard. Commit to working through misunderstandings and walking away with a greater awareness of how you can love your friends better than you did before, despite and even because of your differences. Who knows what God will do through your friends and your mutual decision to choose unity over division?

Friendspiration

THANK-YOU CARD TEMPLATE

Hey ____________,

When we did ____________________, I felt ________________________.
Your _____________ always makes me __________________________.
I respect your ____________________________________ and value
your _____________________. My current season would not be
the same without your ______________________________.
Thank you for being _________________. Here's to more
________________ this year.

Love,

____

Reflect

Have you experienced a friendship conflict that went well? What were some of the communication patterns that restored the friendship? If you haven't experienced a healthy friendship conflict, what is one thing you might do differently next time?

Prayer

Lord, You are so gracious to me. I want to take Your graciousness and model it in my friendships when we disagree. It can be offensive when someone believes differently than me, especially people I really love. I don't want to be insensitive. I want to listen and try to understand. Give me patience and the wisdom to think through what I can say to bring us together instead of creating more distance. And for the friends I've hurt, bring mutual reconciliation between us. Only You, God, can do this big thing between two friends. Amen.

When a Friend Moves Away

I thank my God in all my remembrance of you, always in every prayer of mine for you all making my prayer with joy, because of your partnership in the gospel from the first day until now.

—PHILIPPIANS 1:3–5, ESV

When a friend decides to pack up her home and move closer to her husband's family, doubt or worry can immediately pop up and nag at the back of your mind: "When she moves, are we going to be as close as we are now? Things certainly won't be the way they've been. Can the friendship survive distance?"

A long-distance friendship requires a type of love that has to be stronger than it is for friends who live close by. When you remove in-person connection, the definition of support needs to be redefined. Supporting a long-distance friend may mean sending care packages, leaving a morning voice message, or making plans to visit. Kindness in a long-distance friendship may look like giving your friend space to make new friends while still saving dates on your calendars for phone chats.

When one of my friends moved to a new city, we spent several months talking every day until she settled into her new surroundings. We did a Bible study over FaceTime, and we made annual visits to each other's city. It was a beautiful time in our friendship. Now our phone calls are fewer, and I haven't seen her in a long time. But I don't love her any less. In fact, I remember our shared experiences with such fondness that it brings a warmth to my heart that carries me until the next time I see her.

I appreciate Paul's sentiment in many of his letters to the local churches he visited. When he remembered the people he had ministered with, the memories brought him joy and helped him continue his personal ministry. Long-distance friends are like that. The friendship might not be the same as it once was, but the impact it has had on our lives does not lessen.

My friend who moved away is still so dear in my heart because her impact changed who I am as a friend. I still try to be like her and remain attentive to new friends the way she always did for me, making me feel like I was the most interesting person in the room. The friendship is not remotely the same as it once was day-to-day, but just one conversation with her can be a balm to my soul when I feel stuck in the friendship situations she is now removed from. Sometimes it's even a benefit to have her wisdom speak into situations she's not closely connected to.

As you connect with your significant long-distance friends, I encourage you to do two things. First, find ways to love them. Send them a gift on their birthday, write them a note when you see them post a new DIY tip on their socials, or plan a visit. Second, release them to navigate their own community. They will not be available to talk every day once they've begun to make new relationships. They might forget your birthday—but maybe they'll send a text the next day to apologize. Entrust the future of these friendships to God. He's capable of using the parts of your friendship that made life meaningful for both of you. Your long-distance friends may feel like home for the rest of your life, no matter where you live. There's a peace in knowing you can always come back together as though you hadn't missed a thing.

Reflect

What are some expectations you have about friendship with long-distance friends? Are they realistic? What are some practical ways you can show your long-distance friends you appreciate them?

Prayer

Lord, thank You for my long-distance friends. There was a season they were like my other half, and now I get to root for them from afar. On the days I really miss them, Lord, be a comfort to my sadness. Give me the peace to be happy for them as they make new friends just as I'd like them to be happy for me. I'm asking You to move mountains to get us together soon. Amen.

Friend Date

HOLIDAY HOMECOMING

MATERIALS: thank-you notes, side dish, additional little gift

PREP TIME: 45–60 minutes

DATE TIME: 2 hours

FRIENDS NEEDED: 1+

How do you maintain long-term friendships? Maybe your friends are former roommates from college, the kid who lived next door when you were five, or the members of the high school theater club. Whoever your best buds might be, chances are you don't all live near each other anymore.

I made many of my closest friends in youth group. We saw each other through the braces phase, the boy band glory, and everything in between. After we left for college, we wanted a way to rekindle our friendships during the Christmas holiday. So we decided to celebrate with a dinner party we fondly dubbed "Holiday Homecoming."

The evening requires:

- finding a date who helps you prepare a dish for the event
- taking embarrassing homecoming-style photos
- sitting down for a carb-loaded dinner (because what do you make for a group of twenty-five besides pasta, pasta, pasta)
- performing a dance with your favorite pop music from high school

Everyone eagerly anticipates Holiday Homecoming because it is our chance to share what's been happening in our lives over the past year. It gives us a time and place to applaud answered prayers and hold one another's hands for things still hoped for. We tease each other about embarrassing memories or congratulate one another on new milestones.

I always leave the evening with sore feet, an empty baking dish, and a full heart. The entire evening feels like an expression of my thankfulness to God for creating these friendships from long ago (or maybe not so long ago).

Your Holiday Homecoming might work better around the Fourth of July or Easter, depending on your friends' locations and schedules. You might even be able to get away for an entire weekend instead of just one evening. No matter what your homecoming looks like, start a text thread now to begin planning a unique way to reconnect with old friends.

Mourning Together

Rejoice with those who rejoice; mourn with those who mourn.
—ROMANS 12:15

My sister-in-law passed away recently, far too soon for her young life. My husband was tasked as the executor of her estate and had to mourn his sister while also trying to fulfill her ceremony requests and closing the details of her life. I did my best to keep our home and three children afloat so he could be free from normal dad duties to take care of the responsibilities.

Being two people in their thirties trying to navigate loss and big checklist items was strange. Amid our grief, friends could have chosen to back off or give us space—after all, it's uncomfortable to ask questions or check in when you've never gone through the hard thing yourself. But instead, they leaned in and came close. Our church created a meal train. A friend gave us a date night so we could cry together without the kids around. Friends took time out of their work schedules to attend the funeral; some even flew across the country to be by my husband's side.

When your friends walk through something that feels uncomfortable for you, how can you lean in instead of backing away? Perhaps your friends are going through infertility, the loss of a parent, being overlooked for a promotion, an unexpected divorce, or a difficult diagnosis—all of which can feel bigger than what you can hold. Of course, the pain seems impossible to hold for friends you love! Grieving tough things is icky and overwhelming. It's hard to know how to talk about it without stirring big emotions or saying something inappropriate. You don't want to just ignore your friends' trials, but you don't necessarily feel prepared to take them on either.

When I don't have words, my next step of faith is prayer. I know I can carry those disappointments and pain to God when my friends don't have the strength to carry their concerns themselves. I can lean in by asking God to intercede for them and to be a source of comfort to them. Fortunately, our prayers don't go unheard. We have a God who sees every tear and sleepless night (see Psalm 56:8). He is near to our broken hearts (see Psalm 34:18). He is a comfort to us in our seasons of suffering so that we can be a comfort to others (see 2 Corinthians 1:4). We are not without help when we feel like we are incapable of caring for hurting friends.

Though we might feel strange stepping in and offering a word of prayer, a meal, childcare, or a ride to an appointment, God has equipped us to support our people. Hopefully we find ourselves drawing near rather than pulling away. Comforting our friends doesn't have to be big or fix all their problems. It's usually the smallest gestures—our presence and care—that make the difference to friends going through unexpected loss or hardship.

For all the good things we share with our friends, we must also be available to mourn with them. And good friends will also mourn with you. When a friend grabs my hand and looks me in the eyes to tell me she is sad for me and with me, I feel accepted in my sensitive state. I may be messy, but I will be okay. Sure, there are some who may turn their backs on their friends when the going gets tough. That's very real. Not everyone has the capacity to walk with others through their hurt. But a true friend will stick around because your sadness is her sadness, and the joy you eventually experience will be her joy too. And then you'll get to share in that joy together.

Friendspiration

ACCEPTING HELP

When you're in a trying season, how do you accept help from your friends? Making a list of things that could be helpful for you during a difficult transition is a great way to communicate with those friends who ask to help. I've learned that it is easiest to give the list to my husband and let him be the one to share so that I feel less bossy and more open to receiving help. I've also learned to say yes more when people do make offers. It can feel a little awkward to accept help when you are a perfectly capable adult. That's not the point. We are letting the hands and feet of others be the hands and feet of Jesus. Start with making a list, and later on you might grow more comfortable with accepting help.

Reflect

In what situations do you feel more comfortable leaning in with friends? How can you challenge yourself to check in more with friends who are going through something difficult?

Prayer

Lord, thank You for blessing me with friends who walked with me through my difficult seasons. Help me remember how they made me feel seen, so I can return the same sentiment when they go through something difficult. Help me be an extension of the comfort You offer, God, and be a friend who cares in the good and the bad times. Amen.

PRAYER OF Gratitude for a Full Season

And now, God, do it again—
bring rains to our drought-stricken lives
So those who planted their crops in despair
will shout "Yes!" at the harvest,
So those who went off with heavy hearts
will come home laughing, with armloads of blessing.

—PSALM 126:4–6, MSG

Lord,

You have blessed me so much that it brings a smile to my lips every time I think about the people You have brought into my life. I know it's been a hard road, but I could not be more grateful for the ups and downs that have led me to this place of deep and genuine friendships. Lord, You truly were working behind the scenes and using every moment of connection to create a real sisterhood of friends for me. Even when I doubted or wanted to give up, You provided for me.

Thank You, Lord, for . . .

- conversations that felt like free counseling sessions,
- dinners that turned into late nights down memory lane,
- friends who joined me at church on Sunday mornings,
- coffee dates with more carbs than actual coffee,
- birthday parties with full guest lists I never thought I would have,
- letters of encouragement from friends I respect,
- walks that increased my endorphins with movement and laughter,
- text threads that turned into inside jokes,
- friends who reciprocate, so I'm not always the one initiating hangouts,
- TV marathons when I didn't feel like going out, but also didn't want to be alone,
- Bible studies with women who challenge me,
- same-season-of-life friends who understand what I'm going through,
- women in different stages of life who stand by me and speak wisdom into my situation,
- opportunities to serve my friends with my spiritual gifts,
- friends I can trust to pray for me and support me,

- someone I can call at any hour of the day,
- friends to celebrate my milestones,
- friends who try new things with me,
- friends who help me clean up after hosting them,
- friends who love me for me,
- friends who are faithful, true, and deep.

Thank You for my friends! Thank You for blessing me with some amazing people! May I not take them for granted but instead find new opportunities to pour into them and have fun with them. You were always good and faithful, God, when I felt down on myself and my ability to have friends. And You are good and faithful today as I see myself and the people around me bloom together. I trust You will be good and faithful tomorrow when I hit bumps in the road with my friends, because I know You are always there for me.

Amen.

CLOSING THOUGHTS

The pursuit of meaningful friendship in every season of life is a sacred assignment from God. There are few greater influences than good friends, and we get to choose how we sow into, tend, nourish, and protect the people we are called to share life with.

I've learned in my most recent decade of being a friend that there is no one-size-fits-all when it comes to friendship. If you feel like you've stalled in your friendships, you can always try a different rhythm. If you feel lonely, try making new connections. If a friend has caused you pain, remember that you have the agency to walk away. You don't have to settle for surface-level friendships, and you can always decide to foster deeper and more authentic connections.

As your friendships cycle through different seasons, may God use all of them to equip you to be a better and truer friend.

THERE IS A TIME FOR EVERYTHING,
and a season for every activity
under the heavens . . .

A time to plant and a time to uproot . . .
a time to tear down and a time to build . . .
a time to search and a time to give up . . .
a time to tear and a time to mend,
a time to be silent and a time to speak . . .

He has made everything beautiful in its time.

—ECCLESIASTES 3:1, 2, 3, 6, 7, 11

INK & WILLOW

An imprint of the Penguin Random House Christian Publishing Group, a division of Penguin Random House LLC

1745 Broadway, New York, NY 10019

inkandwillow.com
penguinrandomhouse.com

Interior illustrations: stock.adobe.com: **Marina Zlochin**, all illustrations throughout the devotional, except **InkMarvel**, leaf border (pages 2, 17, 21, 28, 32, 71, 76, 79, 96, 100, 105, 118, 146, 157, 161, 171), plants (pages 52–53); **Buch & Bee**, fig tree in pot on left (page 1), seedling in pot (page 6); **inspiring.team**, plants and frames (pages 4–5); **Rudzhan**, figure (page 52); **Sarocha**, hanging Pothos plant (pages 62, 164)

Hardcover ISBN 979-8-217-15167-7
Ebook ISBN 979-8-217-15258-2

The Library of Congress catalog record is available at https://lccn.loc.gov/2025025199.

Printed in China

9 8 7 6 5 4 3 2 1

First Edition

The authorized representative in the EU for product safety and compliance is Penguin Random House Ireland, Morrison Chambers, 32 Nassau Street, Dublin D02 YH68, Ireland. https://eu-contact.penguin.ie

BOOK TEAM: Editor: Leslie Calhoun • Production editor: Jessica Choi • Managing editors: Julia Wallace, Ruth Chung • Production manager: Jenn Backe • Art director: Sonia Persad • Copy editor: Lisa Grimenstein • Proofreaders: Carrie Krause, Rachael Clements

Cover illustrations: stock.adobe.com: **Marina Zlochin**, border leaves and cat; **Victory**, center plant; **ATerra**, figures

For details on special quantity discounts for bulk purchases, contact specialmarketscms@penguinrandomhouse.com.